SoulTypes

Robert Norton
Richard Southern

SoulTypes

Decode Your Spiritual DNA to Create a Life of Authenticity, Joy, and Grace

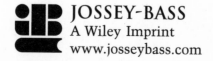

JOSSEY-BASS
A Wiley Imprint
www.josseybass.com

Published by Jossey-Bass
A Wiley Imprint
989 Market Street, San Francisco, CA 94103-1741   www.josseybass.com

Jossey-Bass books and products are available through most bookstores. To contact
Jossey-Bass directly call our Customer Care Department within the U.S. at 800-956-7739,
outside the U.S. at 317-572-3986, or fax 317-572-4002.

Jossey-Bass also publishes its books in a variety of electronic formats. Some content
that appears in print may not be available in electronic books.

The fact that an organization or Website is referred to in this work as a citation and/or
a potential source of further information does not mean that the author or the publisher
endorses the information the organization or Website may provide or recommendations
it may make. Further, readers should be aware that Internet Websites listed in this work
may have changed or disappeared between when this work was written and when it is read.

Credits are on page 169.

Library of Congress Cataloging-in-Publication Data
Norton, Robert, date.
SoulTypes: decode your spiritual DNA to create a life of
authenticity, joy, and grace / Robert Norton and Richard Southern.—
1st ed.
p. cm.
Includes bibliographical references and index.
ISBN 0-7879-6872-2 (alk. paper)
1. Spiritual life—Christianity. I. Southern, Richard, date.
II. Title.
BV4501.3.N67 2004
248.4—dc22   2003022070

Printed in the United States of America
FIRST EDITION
PB Printing 10 9 8 7 6 5 4 3 2 1

CONTENTS

Preface   ix

Acknowledgments   xiii

Introduction: Cracking Your Soul's Code   xv

PART I
Wired for God
Discovering Your Spiritual DNA

1. The Inescapable Conclusion:
   You're Wired for God!   3

2. Who Are You? Discovering
   Your Spiritual Identity   13

3. What's Important to You? Identifying
   Your Core Values   23

4. Why Are You Here? Finding Your
   Unique Life's Purpose   37

5. Where Do You Want to Go in Your Life?
   Creating Your Vision for the Future   51

PART II
Understanding Your Soul Type
Assessments and Practices

6. Heart-Centered Spirituality:
   The Practice of Gratitude   67

7. Soul-Centered Spirituality:
   The Practice of Contemplation   79

8. Mind-Centered Spirituality:
   The Practice of Awareness   99

9. Strength-Centered Spirituality:
   The Practice of Commitment   117

PART III
I Know Where I'm Going
Your Life Map

10. Constructing Your Life Map   133

Epilogue: Follow Your Bliss!   149

Resources   151
Bibliography   155
The Authors   161
Index   163

PREFACE

The concept for this book came out of our professional work with spiritual communities. We were engaged with a "vision team" of a spiritual community in Florida; a young, enthusiastic couple on the team were particularly excited about the principles we were presenting. In fact, they "borrowed" and applied our strategic mapping processes to themselves as a couple; then, pleased with the results they got, they applied them with their children. In both cases, a remarkable transformation came about. First, their marriage, which was shaky at the time, developed into a solid and loving relationship. Then their relationships with their children improved. When they told us about it, we began to see the possibilities for "individualizing" our corporate processes.

We soon heard from others who were doing the same thing. They asked us to consider adapting the processes more specifically for individual use. We added the idea of soul types and related practices to the individual process. When we discussed the total concept with friends and colleagues, the increasingly positive feedback we got was encouraging, so we decided to put the material in a more easily used form.

This book is intended as a practical way to discern your spiritual DNA, determine your soul type, and learn simple ways to put that information to use in experiencing a fuller, more joyful life.

THE STRUCTURE OF THE BOOK

To assist you in this process of self-discovery, we've structured the book in three parts. We begin with an Introduction that gives you an overview of the ideas that have led many (including scientists) to conclude that the sacred can be seen in each of us, and that what is sacred is displayed in a unique way through each of us.

In the three parts, we look at the key elements of cracking your individual spiritual code and discovering the appropriate way—through your soul type—to best reflect your spiritual DNA.

In Part One, we look at key elements that make up the core, the nucleus, of any spiritual DNA. Specifically, this refers to understanding your values, your purpose, and your vision—three components that are fundamental to an understanding of your spiritual DNA.

Part Two examines four ways to express your core spiritual identity through soul types and the practices associated with each type. We present assessments to help you find the soul type that best represents you.

In Part Three, we pull all the skeins together and give you practical suggestions about how to create your own Life Map to guide you into a new future.

A NOTE ON NOTES

This is intended to be a user-friendly book, so we have omitted footnotes in the text. We have, however, provided useful information in the Resources section and in the Bibliography to expand your knowledge about topics that are central to the concept of a spiritual DNA and soul types.

SCRIPTURE QUOTATIONS

The majority of scripture quotes are from *The Holy Bible: Contemporary English Version*, published by the American Bible Society

(1995); and from Eugene Peterson's excellent work *The Message: The Bible in Contemporary English*, published by NavPress (2002). Quotes from other sources are from *World Scripture*, published by the International Religious Foundation (1995).

This book is lovingly dedicated to our mothers
Frances Marie Southern and Dorothy McGregor Norton
who imparted to us our DNA—
both physical and spiritual.
We are grateful to you.

ACKNOWLEDGMENTS

The crunch comes for writers when you submit your book proposal, hold your breath, cross your fingers, and wait. We submitted ours to Sheryl Fullerton, executive editor of the Religion in Practice Series for Jossey-Bass in San Francisco. Fortunately for us, Sheryl and her colleagues gave us a quick response and—best of all—a green light of acceptance. A proposal is relatively easy to craft; a manuscript, on the other hand, is challenging to write. But we were fortunate to use the services of Naomi Lucks, a freelance development editor and wonder worker. Because of Sheryl—every author's dream editor— her excellent staff, and Naomi, this book has been possible.

INTRODUCTION

Cracking Your Soul's Code

"If there is no meaning," said the king, "that saves a world of trouble, you know, as we needn't try to find any."
LEWIS CARROLL

Our view of the world can change in a moment. When the first pictures of the earth as seen from space were shown on television and printed in magazines, the images moved philosophic speculations about the interdependence and interconnectedness of all creation to a new level. The astounding image of our earth as a spinning blue-and-green ball in the darkness of space underscored the call of the great Swiss pioneer psychoanalyst Carl Jung for a new "myth," a new paradigm, a new spirituality that encompasses the realities of the world in which we live, yet honors the wisdom of the past.

Robert Wuthnow, the prominent sociologist of religion at Princeton University, argues in his book *After Heaven* that this new kind of spirituality must not simply be *seeker spirituality*, with its emphasis on fluidity; nor should it continue to focus on *dwelling spirituality*, with its emphasis on institutional rules and predefined doctrine. Wuthnow, much like Jung, sees the need for a new *practice spirituality* that incorporates all elements of our being and emphasizes how we live out our spiritual types.

Our own conclusion, after working with thousands of people of faith, is that Wuthnow is spot on. We can create a new practice of spirituality *and* honor our older religious traditions.

It's like the old joke: "Excuse me, sir," a visitor to Manhattan asked a man on the street, "Can you tell me how to get to Carnegie Hall?" The man replied, "Certainly, young man. Practice, practice, practice!" *Which* practice, of course, is up to you; there is no single spiritual practice that answers all of one's longing for God. Spirituality is a single journey with many highways, and the range of practices varies as much as individual needs do. The human species may be one family, but it has many faces.

THE FOUR SOUL TYPES

We humans have always had a desire to fit people into categories, from the many methods of astrology to phrenology, and in contemporary times, to the Enneagram, the Myers-Briggs Type Indicator for personality, and spiritual type assessments. We search for ways to understand our hidden values in a spiritual context.

We live today in a technologically advanced society, yet finding meaning in life continues to be an important quest. We believe the advances of the contemporary world and the concomitant rise in religious and spiritual exploration are wonderfully complementary; the work of both strengthens the search for meaning. In particular, we have been profoundly inspired by the Human Genome Project, which has undertaken the enormous goal of identifying and mapping all of the approximately thirty thousand genes in human DNA—cracking the code of life. This work offers intriguing insights, and it led us to wonder: Is it possible to uncover equally significant insights about a "spiritual DNA," the soul's code? We believe it is. In this book we explore how you can crack your soul's code, decode and identify your soul type, and use that information to map your vision for the future. This approach has two important components: analyzing the concept of the soul, and uncovering the critical information embedded in it—the spiritual DNA. To learn more about our spiritual DNA, we must ask four perennial questions:

1. Who am I? What is my authentic identity?

2. What's important to me? What are my values, my gifts, my passions?

3. Why am I here? What is my purpose or mission in life?

4. Where am I going? What is my vision of my future?

Using the processes in this book, you will find your own unique answer for these questions. Then you can turn to a fifth crucial question:

5. How do I get from where I am to where I want to be?

To answer this last question, you will create a map that guides you as you navigate your life's path.

The approach we've taken in this book is to identify *soul types* that are based on one's spiritual DNA and the expression, or practice, of it. Our framework for soul types is found in Jesus' answer to the question posed to him by a legal scholar, "Teacher, which commandment in the law is the greatest?" Jesus replied, "You must love God with all your heart, soul, mind, and strength. The second most important commandment says, 'Love others as much as you love yourself.' No other commandment is more important than these" (Mark 12:28–29).

Love, then, is the key to experiencing life fully. It is insightful to note that Jesus could have simply replied, "Love God," and that would have been a satisfactory answer. But he was not willing to leave it there. Love, he said, must be worked out in everyday living in a variety of ways, so he delineated four interrelated, interdependent spiritualities: heart, soul, mind, and strength. These are the bases of the four soul types we explore in this book.

The four soul types are not mutually exclusive. We can find God in each of these spiritualities, and the four are within all of us.

Preference, however, is another issue. Your preference in relation to the practices that define these spiritualities determines your soul type:

1. *Heart-centered*. "Love God with all your heart." This spirituality is primarily displayed through the practice of *gratitude*.

2. *Soul-centered*. "Love God with all your soul." This spirituality of the inner life is primarily seen in the practice of *contemplation*.

3. *Mind-centered*. "Love God with all your mind." This spirituality is primarily expressed through the practice of *awareness*.

4. *Strength-centered*. "Love God with all your strength." This spirituality is primarily exemplified through the practice of *commitment*.

Please note that the operative and consistent word in each practice is the same: *all*. Jesus has given us a holistic model, four distinct ways to love God, four distinct ways to practice that love—but they are all interdependent and interrelated. You may favor one over the other, but it still takes all four to make up the whole.

WHAT IS YOUR SOUL'S CODE?

In this book, you learn to discover your spiritual DNA and crack your soul's code. This is work of the self-inquiring sort: we ask you to reflect on questions designed to uncover your deepest way of being. For this journey, you will need a journal (or a good supply of paper) and a quiet place to reflect.

The work you do in Part One helps you discover your spiritual DNA by answering the questions we posed earlier: Who am I? What's important to me? Where am I going? What is my vision for the future? How will I get there?

In Part Two, you discover your soul type and learn specific practices to help you reinforce this spiritual dimension.

Part Three is the culmination of all the work you do in this process: constructing your Life Map from the information you have learned about your authentic self. This map is not only a practical way to express your uniqueness but also a way to create and live life goals and objectives on the basis of your soul type and your own unique spiritual DNA.

Blessings on your journey!

SoulTypes

PART I

Wired for God

Discovering Your Spiritual DNA

Imagine
Be who you are
Practice what you know
Teach what you learn
And continue to grow
Just imagine!
Just imagine that
You are smarter than you know
More courageous than you guess
Stronger than you feel
Healthier than you are aware of
More creative than you believe
More capable than you recognize
You are more powerful than you think
More attractive than you assume
Wiser than you suppose
More valuable than you have ever been told
And you are able to make a difference in the world
That you have not yet begun to realize
Just imagine!

Author unknown

magine" is a glimpse of the theme that runs throughout Part One, that you are more than you know, and more than you imagine yourself to be.

Through the chapters in Part One, you'll explore your true identity as a living being gifted by the source of life with a spiritual code that is absolutely unique to you. This code can be discovered, understood, and utilized, so why not identify and use it for your highest good?

Whether you are a spiritual seeker, a rational scientific type, or a bit of both, there is a growing interest in understanding this code and what it reveals about you and your relationship with that which is greater than you.

1

The Inescapable Conclusion

You're Wired for God!

All are but parts of one stupendous whole
Whose body Nature is, and God is the soul.
ALEXANDER POPE

Whether we describe ourselves as religious or spiritual or both, most of us feel that God is genuinely involved in our lives in some personal way. The spiritual life is essentially a learning experience in which we examine situations, challenges, and relationships in the effort to discern a message worth learning or sharing with others. We are often looking for a way to make what we do count—to make a difference.

As a seeker on a spiritual journey, your purpose is to move toward living in awareness of the presence of God. As you travel life's journey, every mountain you climb, every valley you pass through, every river you cross brings you closer to God. This journey is not only for great sages and gurus; it's for everyone. Spirituality, as historian of religions Huston Smith has said, is living the ordinary life in an extraordinary way.

SCIENCE AND RELIGION: IS CONVERGENCE HAPPENING?

The religious community has always accepted that from the smallest particle to the whole of the universe, there is a divine blueprint throughout nature. Science, they say, may give us theories and even proof of how the cosmos works, but the great religions have always taught that a higher intelligence both created and sustains the universe. God's grand design is the foundation for the very life within us all. But until relatively recently, the scientific community largely dismissed such metaphysical speculations because they couldn't be scientifically proven. Even so, there were those who continued their deep longing to connect with something greater than themselves. Thus, despite sages and prognosticators, the sacred didn't go away— not even for rational scientists.

The medieval philosopher-scientist Moses Maimonides said that not only is science the surest way of knowing God, it is the only way. Down through the centuries he would be joined by other scientists, notably Nicholas Copernicus, Francis Bacon, Galileo Galilee, Johannes Kepler, Isaac Newton, and Albert Einstein, each spiritual in his own way. Though Einstein was not religious in the accepted sense, he was quoted (in his *New York Times* obituary, on April 19, 1955) as saying, "True religion is real living; living with all one's soul, with all one's goodness and righteousness." If that isn't spiritual, what is?

Science cannot be advanced without observation, without seeing patterns, without being aware; neither can spirituality. Scientists today are continuing to discover new evidence that supports an ancient belief central to most of the world's religions: that there is a grand design to all creation.

IS GOD HARDWIRED INTO THE HUMAN BRAIN?

Now, the work of Dr. Andrew Newberg, a radiologist at the University of Pennsylvania, suggests a startling idea: humans are innately structured to believe in God. To put it another way, God is hardwired into the human brain!

Newberg has developed a biological theory that says there is a neurological basis for the great human hunger for God. This theory has made him a leading figure in the emerging science of *neuro-theology*, which explores the link between spirituality and the brain. Newberg's research is based on work begun in the 1970s by the psychiatrist and anthropologist Eugene d'Aquili, who theorized that brain functions were capable of producing religious experiences, ranging from the most profound spiritual experience of mystical union with God to the quiet sense of holiness one feels at prayer.

Newberg and d'Aquili teamed up in the 1990s. Together, they worked to refine and test the latter's theory, using imaging technology to map the brains of Tibetan Buddhist monks deep in meditation and Franciscan nuns in deep contemplative prayer. The photographic results appeared to be pictures of the brain in a state of mystical transcendence. Newberg and d'Aquili discovered that intense spiritual contemplation triggers an alteration in the activity of the brain that leads us to perceive transcendent religious experience as solid and tangibly real. So what the Buddhist monks call "oneness with the universe," and the Franciscan nuns call "the palpable presence of God," is not delusional wishful thinking but a series of neurological events that can be objectively observed, recorded, and photographed.

Vince Rause interviewed Newberg and wrote a compelling article, "The Science of God: Searching for the Divine":

> Newberg tells me something I'm not sure I can grasp: that the fabled "higher reality" described by mystics might, in fact, be real.
>
> "You mean *figuratively* real," I say with a troubled squint.
>
> "No," he says, "As real as this table. More real, in fact."
>
> "You're saying your research proved this higher reality exists?" I ask.
>
> "I'm saying the possibility of such a reality is not inconsistent with science," he says.
>
> "But you can't observe such a thing in a scientific way, can you?"

Newberg grins. He hasn't simply observed such a state; he has managed to take its picture.

"Does this mean that God is just a perception generated by the brain, or has the brain been wired to experience the reality of God?" I ask.

"The best and most rational answer I can give to both questions," Newberg answers, "is yes."

Their research suggests that all these feelings are rooted not in emotion or wishful thinking but in the genetically arranged wiring of the brain.

"Religion thrives in an age of reason," Newberg says.

God is hard-wired into the human brain! This new and exciting possibility is what the soul has always known: that we have an innate yearning for a relationship with God.

The Human Genome Project is another amazing scientific breakthrough that we see as having spiritual implications. The Genome Project has indexed, through the combined efforts of great scientific minds and supercomputers, the string of our genetic code—the four letters A, G, C, T—in almost infinite combinations. As a result, we have the beginning blueprint of how our human organisms are formed and how they grow. This major milestone anticipates medical miracles, cures for what previously was incurable, and palliative measures that still lie ahead.

The implications of these scientific breakthroughs initiate confirmation that the spiritual journey is neither a figment of imagination nor an escape from reality, but a natural outcome of the search for who we are as human beings.

YOUR SOUL'S CODE

Just as physical DNA determines much of your life direction, your spiritual DNA—which is embedded in the soul—affects the path that you take as a seeker on your spiritual journey. We all share many commonalities, but our exact needs vary, and we each express our spiritual DNA differently. "When I speak of 'spiritual DNA,'" author Julia Cameron writes, "I am talking about a stamp of originality that is as definite and specific as my blue eyes, blond hair, medium height. Just as our physical potentials are encoded at conception, it is my belief that we also carry the imprint, or blueprint, of our gifts and their unfolding."

Discovering your spiritual DNA allows you to decode your life: to understand the distinctiveness of who you are and what God has called you to be and do. By understanding your spiritual DNA, you step across a threshold to a new spiritual life. Enjoy the newness of this moment of spiritual discovery, enjoy the curious mixture of serenity and intense excitement as the Spirit stirs in your soul. This is your moment with God.

Cracking your soul's code begins by answering these five questions:

1. Who am I?
2. What's important to me?
3. Why am I here?
4. Where do I want to go in my life?
5. How do I get there?

Finding these answers will occupy you for the better part of this book. This is a thoughtful and reflective task, and we ask you to take as much time and care as you need.

Once you have your answers, you are better able to identify your soul type, which is based on Jesus' instruction to love God with all your heart, all your soul, all your mind, and all your strength. We explore these four types in more depth in Part Two, but right now let's look at each one to get a taste of what lies ahead on your path.

The *heart-centered* soul type experiences life in the here and now and embraces it as something to be lived with feeling and emotion.

These people may have experienced some life-changing, transformative moment of emotion, of feeling, of knowing that all is well with the world. The same heart-changing experience is found in all the living traditions, which tells us that heart spirituality is a primary form of spirituality for millions of people.

The *soul-centered* soul type seeks transformation through strengthening the interior life, to become one with the source of life. When Jesus withdrew into the desert to be alone with God, he was demonstrating this spirituality. The ongoing popularity of meditation in all the great religious traditions stands witness to the fact that many people are attracted to this form of practice. There is growing interest in centering prayer, in walking the labyrinth, in simply being aware of one's breath, all practices that confirm the power of this spirituality.

The *mind-centered* soul type is exemplified by the Greek philosopher Plato, who recorded Socrates' famous statement that "the unexamined life is not worth living." An unexamined life is almost unimaginable for those who are on this path. Thinking, reasoning, learning, questioning, and doubting are all positive words in mind-centered spirituality.

Recall the touching pictures of Mother Teresa comforting the dying poor of India, or the pictures of Diana, Princess of Wales, wearing protective gear as she walked through a devastated landscape embedded with land mines; these are examples of the *strength-centered* soul type. These are two names and lives that are publicly celebrated, but there are millions more, unknown for the most part, who have found God through this commitment to serving others with all their strength.

THE SPIRITUAL JOURNEY

Once you've cracked your code and discerned your soul type, you'll pull it all together in the form of a Life Map. Your map shows you ways to stay on course in your spiritual journey. The idea of a spiritual journey is far from new. In fact, this theme is reflected in many traditions and is worth reflecting on before we set out.

The Indian sage Sri Aurobindo reminds us that the spiritual journey entails discipline, courage, and perseverance. "The spiritual journey," he said, "is one of continuously falling on your face, getting up, brushing yourself off, looking sheepishly at God and taking another step."

When a monk asked Master Unmon, "What is the Tao?" the Master cryptically replied, "Move on, it's important to keep moving."

Confucius said that it does not matter how slowly you go, so long as you don't stop.

The people of Israel wandered for forty years in the wilderness before finally reaching the Promised Land.

Jesus led his followers across the length and breadth of Palestine in their teaching missions.

Paul of Tarsus, the Book of Acts says, was converted while traveling on the road to Damascus.

Muslims have an obligation to journey to Mecca at least once in their lives.

Trappist monk Thomas Merton says, "Our real journey in life is *interior*; it is a matter of growth, deepening, and of an ever greater surrender to the creative action of love and grace in our hearts."

Sociologist Wade Clark Roof brought this journey theme closer to home in his address to a conference of journalists, when he observed that the auto industry is replete with "journey" names for their SUVs. Roof said that these choices "illustrate a searching mood in society: 'Voyager,' 'Explorer,' 'Discovery,' 'Quest,' 'Expedition,' and 'Odyssey.'" If we are spiritual beings on a human path rather than human beings on a spiritual path, then life is not simply getting from one place to the next, it's a pilgrimage and a quest.

Spirituality has a transcendent quality that opens us up to many forms and concepts. Characterized by wonder, mystery, and awe, spirituality is an inner experience that goes beyond the external boundaries of organized religion and church doctrine. Lama Surya Das writes: "The renewed public interest in spirituality of all kinds, wherever it may be found, is a natural expression of our shared long-ing for freedom and truth, for inner peace, joy, and fulfillment."

Spirituality can be defined in many ways. Psychiatrist Gerald May refers to it as the deep values and desires that are at the cen-ter of our being. Seminary professor Corinne Ware sees it as con-necting with God and with each other. Author Ellen Bass says, "There is a part of every living thing that wants to become itself, the tadpole into the frog, the chrysalis into the butterfly, a damaged human being into a whole one. That is spirituality."

Like religion, spirituality is a web that holds us together and connects us to something greater than ourselves.

■ ■ ■

As you walk through the Louvre, in Paris, your attention may be drawn to a marble fireplace in a small, paneled room. Actually, it's a connecting passage between the rooms that house some of the great works of art. It's easy to walk past this fireplace, but it's so exquisite that once you've noticed it you feel compelled to stop for a closer look. A frieze runs across the face of it under the ledge. Seen from a distance, it seems to be a scene painted directly on the marble. But closer inspection reveals it to be a mosaic made up of thousands of tiny tiles of different sizes, shapes, and hues, painstakingly cut and arranged to form a complete picture.

You can think of your spiritual life in the same way: as a mosaic made up of people you've known, experiences you've had, beliefs you hold, and places you've been. God is the source of all these pieces, but you get to choose and put the pieces in their place as you create your own life's mosaic.

You begin your journey with the first step: discovering who you are.

Life Map Notes

Throughout this book, beginning in the next chapter, we ask you to get out your journal or a pad of paper and reflect on questions about yourself. Please keep these notes with the book as you read it; you will need them when you create your Life Map in Chapter Ten.

2

Who Are You?

Discovering Your Spiritual Identity

Look for it and you will find it—what is unsought will go undetected.
SOPHOCLES

Two friends, Mike and Frankie, were walking near a lake on a quiet afternoon. Mike says, "You know, no one's around, so why don't we do some skinny dipping?"

"Sounds good," Frankie replies, "but I have a problem. I'll have to take off all my clothes to skinny dip, so how will I know who I am when I get out of the water?"

"Hmmm," says Mike, mulling over the problem. "I've got it. Here, I have a piece of blue twine in my pocket, we'll tie it around your big toe, so when you come out of the water, you'll know who you are."

They agreed and the twine was tied. But while they were swimming, the twine slipped off Frankie's toe and wrapped itself around Mike's toe. When they came out of the water, Frankie looked down at his toe, and the blue twine was missing. Then he saw that the blue twine was tied around Mike's big toe. Flabbergasted, Frankie said to Mike: "I know who you are, but who am I?"

Versions of this story are found in many traditions and cultures. They all make the point that "Who am I?" is an important question that can only be answered by each individual. Yet most people live in a fog about their spiritual identity; they put energy and time into other things that distract them from answering this simple but fundamental question.

13

ARE YOU YOUR SOUL?

The *Titanic* disaster, on April 14, 1912, was heralded by a headline that read, "Titanic Sinks: 1,620 Souls Lost at Sea." This headline presupposed a common acceptance of what a soul is. Actually, there was not then, nor is there now, a universally accepted definition of soul.

Many believe that you're born with your soul, and when you die it dies with you. Others say your soul lives on beyond your physical death. Still others feel that your soul is preexistent and enters your body at conception, or at birth, and when you die it travels on to another body, before reaching total union with God. Some argue that your soul is the real essence of your being, and that your body is nothing more than a vehicle for your soul. Some say your body is simply an outer expression of your soul within, while others insist that your soul and body are fused together to form you as a complete being.

All living religious traditions have something to say about the concept of the soul. Hindus refer to an individual soul as the *atman*, or the highest self, a part of God, an expression of God—which, in reality, is God. Sri Aurobindo said the soul is an alive, evolving, psychic being; that once it understands its connection to cosmic consciousness, the soul displays not only its unique individuality but also its relationship to the totality of being.

Buddhists, on the other hand, have no teaching about a deity or creator god, so there is no affirmation of a separate soul and no individual expression of the divine. They see the concept of a separate soul as an expression of clinging to the self. For Buddhists, the purpose of discovering your spiritual DNA would be to assist you in realizing your true nature, an effort that typically requires a focused and disciplined mind.

In the Hebrew scriptures, the Book of Genesis relates that God formed the human race from the dust of the earth; when God breathed life into humankind, we became living souls. The essential dichotomy of seeing humanity as both soul and body gave Judaism a holistic understanding of individual existence.

According to Sufi teachings, your soul, or *ruh*, is connected to God—even if you are not conscious of the connection—at seven soul levels: mineral, vegetable, animal, personal, human, secret, and inner secret, with unique gifts and skills for each level. By conscious development you can express these gifts for your personal benefit and for society. Your soul, Sufis say, goes through an evolutionary process as it grows through these levels, until finally it reaches a holistic state in which it encompasses all aspects of your individuality: mind, body, and spirit.

Christianity uses the Greek word *psyche* for soul more than one hundred times in the New Testament, indicating a number of understandings of the concept. Rather than a separate, immortal soul, the central theme here is that your soul is *one aspect* of your individual identity, which will be restored at the resurrection. In the formative days of Christian teaching, St. Augustine's concept that the soul is the image of God was widely accepted. By the medieval period, the soul was referred to as "the echo of the body," in which soul had some connection with God and yet maintained its own separateness. The Protestant Reformation brought a strongly rational view of humans as having a dichotomy of body and soul as two separate spheres of being. Today we see a decided shift back to a unitary concept of mind, body, and spirit.

Clearly, there are many definitions for soul!

In this book, when we speak of the soul we mean the organizing principle for an individual life, which can be perceived and expressed in a variety of ways: through the mind, through the affect, through silence, and through activity. Whatever the origin of the soul—or the origin of the concept of the soul—the fact is that from a spiritual perspective you're created in love, sustained in love, and called to love. In this sense, soul is, as Huston Smith has said, "the final locus of our individuality."

WHAT'S IN A NAME?

Names are intended to distinguish individuals from one another. Imagine how difficult it would be if we did not use names. Instead of saying "Marie," for example, one would have to say something like "the beautiful blond woman who lives in the green house down the street"!

Names are convenient. Some names carry information about roots, such as inherited family, clan, or tribal names. If you look in the phone directory, you'll see many listings for a common last name such as Jones or Lopez or Wong.

Names can serve other purposes as well. The Chinese use names to identify the generation of the bearer. African cultures use names to describe the order in which siblings are born. Given names (first names) are generally bestowed at some point after the birth of a child, or they are decided upon before birth.

 Life Map Notes: What's in Your Name?

1. Print your first name (or middle name, if you go by that) here (or, preferably, in your journal): _____

2. If you're known by a nickname, print it here: _____

3. Have you ever been identified by a negative name? Did you buy into it at the time? _____

If you find the process of naming particularly intriguing, explore these optional questions.

4. What is the etymology (derivation) of your given name?

To research the meaning of your name, search the Internet using the keywords "names," "meaning of names," "etymology." You'll be able to research names from most cultures. If your name was specially created for you, you probably won't find it; however, you might find a name that sounds like yours and probably has a similar meaning. For example: Donna means "lady" in Italian. Jeffrey or Geoffrey, a variant of Godfrey, means "peace of God."

5. What does your surname (last name) mean?

You can also search the Internet using the keyword "genealogy" for the meaning of your last name. For example, Williams is from Wilhelm, composed of *will* ("will," "desire") and *helm* ("helmet," "protection").

6. Do you feel you fit your name?   ❑ Yes   ❑ No

7. If you were to change your name, what would you choose?

Would you choose it just because you like it, or because you've researched the etymology and you find that the derivation fits you?

Negative Names Are Not Who We Are

Sometimes people are identified by negative nicknames that are suggestive of mistakes, low self-image, or physical attributes (Klutz, Lazybones, Slut, Fatty, Four Eyes). . . . We hope you do not identify with any of these or other such names; but if you do, remember that such a name is not who you really are. The great traditions got it right by bestowing positive names such as "God's own," "God's creation," "my beloved," "precious child," "chosen," and "friend." In these teachings, God sees you as very valuable.

Overcoming Negative Names

Long ago, a mother suffered great pain in childbirth. To punish her son for her agony, she named him Jabez (pronounced jay-bez), which in Hebrew means "born in pain." It makes you think twice before assigning names to kids, doesn't it?

Very little is known about Jabez. His great accomplishment is that he made it into the pages of sacred scripture. His "story" is briefly told in 1 Chronicles 4:9–11, buried in a list of long-forgotten people. What we do know is that he turned his negative name into a positive, and he created a simple prayer said by millions of people each day. It's a prayer for healing, abundance, creativity, and blessing, a prayer that serves as a reminder that whatever you are called you are a child of God, and you deserve the best. Here's his one-sentence contribution to the world:

> Jabez called on the God of Israel, saying "Oh, that you would bless me indeed and enlarge my territory, that your hand would be with me, and that you would keep me from evil, that I may not cause pain." And God granted his request.

In our own time, there's a young woman who wouldn't let herself be named "homeless." On the basis of her early life circumstances, Lauralee Summer would have been prejudged a loser with little or no chance of success. She grew up homeless, with a single mom who struggled each day just to find a place to stay, food to eat, and secondhand clothes for herself and her daughter. Their days were spent living on the streets and sleeping in shelters or welfare hotels. Like many homeless, they moved frequently: California, Arizona, Oregon, and finally across the continent to Massachusetts. Lauralee grew up with few expectations and little security. Yet she had an enormous reserve of inner strength, and she learned to love reading. Through books, she was able to get beyond appearances and began to find her true self. In Boston, while they were living in a shelter, she enrolled in high school.

As Lauralee became more self-aware, and as her life settled into a pattern, her views of herself changed and her academic scores soared to the honor level. Her self-confidence reached the point where she made up her mind to be the first girl to compete on the boys' wrestling team! This was the stuff of dreams for the media, and the nation began to hear about her. By the time she appeared on *Good Morning America* and had been featured in *People* magazine, millions knew about Lauralee Summer, the girl raised in homeless shelters who was accepted into Harvard University.

Lauralee is now twenty-five, a graduate of Harvard, no longer homeless, and working on an advanced degree at the University of California at Berkeley, studying children's literature. From homeless to Harvard is a winning theme; she has sold her life story to a major publishing house for a substantial retainer—and she's sold the movie rights, too. How did all this rags-to-riches stuff actually happen? Lauralee said in an interview with the *San Francisco Chronicle*, "When you can never expect what you'll see next or what life's going to be like, it makes it easier to try new things. Would I want a home? The feeling of home is just getting to know yourself."

Actor Christopher Reeve, who played the role of *Superman* in several films, knows who he is. Superman, you recall, is the superhuman guy from the planet Krypton who is faster than a speeding bullet and can use his X-ray vision to look through walls of steel. Reeve, who played in other films as well, was at the top of his acting game when he fell off his horse and suffered total paralysis of his body. Now, instead of "leaping over tall buildings in a single bound," he is confined to a motorized wheelchair and must speak with the aid of a breathing tube. Is his life over? Not at all. He didn't define his life by his career, and he will not be defined as handicapped. Though he can't use his talents in the old way, he's capitalized on his prominence to become a strong advocate for disabled people. Christopher Reeve is clear about his identity.

WHAT ABOUT GOD'S NAME?

Even God has been assigned names by others. Did you know that "God" is not God's name? Are you also aware there are an infinite number of names for God?

The character Pope Xystus I in the play *The Ring* says, "God is not the name of God, but an opinion about God." It's probable that no one actually knows what the sacred name is, but this hasn't stopped people from searching for it and, in the meantime, deciding what to call God.

The divine name was so sacred to ancient Hebrews that it was never to be uttered, so when they wrote it they left out the vowels, which produced "YHWH." Scholars use the Greek term *tetragrammaton*, which means four letters, to describe this usage. The missing vowels are probably *a* and *e*, so that the sacred name for Jews and Christians is most likely "Yahweh," but we're so used to saying "God" there hasn't been much of a move to switch to Yahweh. In the scriptures the first basic name for God is "Elohim," which is a variant of *El* (the godhead) in Semitic languages. Ancient Ugaritic used *El*, and in Babylonian it was *Ilu*, and in Arabic, *Allah*.

Other religions and cultures have their own names for God. In Islam, in addition to Allah there are at least ninety-nine names for the one God. Hindus can multiply that by ten plus one and claim at least a thousand Sanskrit names for the sacred, each name having its own special meaning. Christian Science and many New Thought philosophies refer to God as "Mind," "Spirit," "Soul," "Principle," "Life," "Truth," and "Love." Masonic writings refer to God as "TGAOTU," The Great Architect of the Universe. Native Americans invoked God as the "Great Spirit," and "Manitou." Alcoholics Anonymous and related support groups don't use the word *God* but prefer the more generic term "Higher Power." They do this because some people either have been (or perceive that they have been) wounded by others in God's name.

So since no one really knows what God's name is—if, indeed, God has or needs a name—we have the option of using whatever name or term we find fits us best. In this book, we have used God, but you are welcome to mentally substitute any other word.

Here are some other names and terms for God that we've come across (and you can probably add a few more): Infinite, Source, Divine Energy, Uncaused Cause, Spirit, Ground of All Being, One Life, Universe, Divine Mind, Divine Thought, Infinite Love, Changeless One, Prime Mover, Father-Mother, Presence, Absolute, Creator, Sustainer, Redeemer, Universal Flow, Radiant Light.

THE POWER OF NAMES

We had an excellent experience of the power of names when we visited the Provincial Museum of Alberta in Edmonton, Canada, which was hosting a special exhibit: "Anno Domini: Jesus Through the Centuries—Exploring the Heart of Two Millennia." According to the catalogue, it was a "glimpse [of] some of the ways Jesus has been understood and how this understanding has shaped and reshaped culture."

Entering the exhibit area, we were confronted by a curved wall with the question, "Who do you say that I am?" emblazoned in large letters. Surrounding the question were short answers, including Savior, Rabbi, Teacher, Poet, Cosmic Christ, King of Kings, and Son of Man. The exhibit focused on presenting the answers to the question, yet retaining the centrality of the person of Jesus. Each response was displayed in its own space and with its own theme: "Turning Point of History," "Light of Gentiles," "King of Kings," "Cosmic Christ," "Son of Man," "True Image," "Monk Who Rules the World," "Bridegroom of the Soul," "Divine and Human Model," "The Universal Man," "Mirror of the Eternal," "Prince of Peace," "Teacher of Common Sense," "Poet of the Spirit," "Liberator," and, finally, "Man Who Belongs to the World."

Each display was a "snapshot" featuring ancient and contemporary works of art and artifacts, with contemporary and ancient quotations. So we, and the other visitors—many of whom were from diverse religious traditions—were confronted with a variety of ways that artists and others experienced Jesus, according to their concepts of him. Probably most of the visitors had previously been exposed to a single view of Jesus. When they found a particular area of the exhibit that best fit their picture, they felt comfortable, but not so comfortable in other areas. We listened carefully to people's comments.

One woman was thrilled over the "Jesus, the King of Kings" display; another, with the concept of Jesus as "Cosmic Christ." Several people found "Jesus, the Teacher of Common Sense," to be their favorite model. Still others rejoiced at the display of "Jesus, the True Image." One man said, "I never realized that there were so many ways to see Jesus." His wife commented, "It's like there's one Jesus, but many faces of him." As people worked their way through the exhibit they saw indeed at least eighteen ways to experience Jesus. No doubt there are hundreds of thousands of other names for the sacred from every culture, religion, and tradition on the planet.

Life Map Notes: Sacred Names

My preferred name(s) or term(s) for the sacred: _____

_____

_____

3

What's Important to You?

Identifying Your Core Values

Those who know others are learned.
Those who know themselves are wise.
LAO TZU

Charlene handed the checkout clerk at the supermarket a twenty-dollar bill. The clerk gave the woman her change, and she just slipped it all—bills, change, and receipt—into her pocket. When she got home she was shocked to learn that she'd been given not $8 in change, but $108!

What to do? Her friends pointed out that she certainly could use that extra cash for her kids. The store might be short a hundred dollars at the end of the day, one of them said, but it's small change to them and they'd be sure to make it up somehow. Another reminded her that this would just about offset the times when she and other customers were inadvertently overcharged, or when an item didn't get bagged, and no one from the store tried to track her down and give her the missing item. Anyway, they said, it wasn't her fault, and in the long run it would all balance out.

 Time Out: What's Your Response?

How do you feel about this? What would you have done? Was she a fool for taking all that time over a mistake that wasn't hers?

Charlene's friends, of course, were speaking from their own sense of values and beliefs. But one of her core values was honesty, and she knew she could not be true to herself if she kept the money. How could she proclaim honesty as a value if she, in her own mind, was dishonest? What lesson would that be for her kids? "Honesty is the best policy," she remembered hearing. She took the money back. Well, the store clerk didn't want it, saying to the best of their knowledge no mistake had been made. The woman was insistent. A supervisor had to be called, and they did a time-consuming reconciliation of the cash drawer. It turned out that it had been a very busy day, and some of the bills ended up in the wrong slots. The mystery was solved, the store got its money back, the clerk was very thankful, and Charlene left satisfied. Most important to her was the knowledge that she had successfully lived into one of her core values.

CORE VALUES

Core values are those foundational, deeply rooted beliefs and strengths that establish boundaries and expectations of behavior, impel us to take action, and help us make daily decisions that are consistent with our beliefs. When you know your core values and allow them to establish your personal boundaries, they translate into standards of behavior and expectations. Knowing your core values allows you to live life with ease and grace. If you are not so sure of your core values, you can waste valuable energy just trying to determine what's the "right" thing to do.

Your values say what you are willing to do, and where you draw the line. Firmly held core values are so strong that they endure even when your circumstances change. Your core values, as we saw with Charlene, help you make daily decisions that are consistent with your beliefs. They impart a clear sense of your principles and priorities.

What you value is a good indicator of where you will choose to invest your energies. A person who says *family* is an important value, for example, won't disparage other family members behind their backs. A person who holds up *truth* as a core value doesn't consistently lie. (Mark Twain once said that it was his policy always to tell the truth because that way you don't have so much to remember. He identified truth as a value, and in a broad sense he defined it for himself!)

Understanding your core values impels you to be authentic—true to yourself. Lack of personal authenticity stems from a lack of awareness of the values or beliefs that are at the center of who you are. There is often a great gap between what people say they value and how they actually live. You see, your values are about behavior—*your* behavior, not someone else's—so it's important to separate your dreams about yourself from your reality. Your values get to the heart of what makes you tick, and they reveal themselves in diverse ways. At times of crisis and adversity, they kick in and you respond almost automatically. At those moments you reveal your true self because you are, at that instant, coming from the depths of your soul.

A core value is a positive preference or choice you make throughout the day. It may be spontaneous, unrehearsed, and unpracticed. Your emotional explosions, knee-jerk reactions, snap judgments, and heavy sighs reveal much more of who you are than the masks you've been hiding behind. No one is perfect; we all fail to make proper choices or behave positively from time to time. But if you are truly serious about your core values, when such a moment does happen you'll work to get past the experience and then adjust your lifestyle to bring it into harmony with your values.

STAY CONNECTED TO LIFE

The Quaker philosopher Elton Trueblood once said that no matter how much money you spend on cut flowers, how beautifully you arrange them, or how delicate the fragrance may be, they are dead; they eventually wither and decay because they have been cut off from their life source. Without core values, our lives are as rootless and lifeless as cut flowers. By living your values daily, you form your character. Values are spiritual roots that permit you to bloom. Authentic core values are lasting and enduring; they touch the heart and the emotions; identify what is important to you, including your interests and passions; communicate how you "walk your talk."

LIVING IN HARMONY WITH YOUR CORE VALUES

Living your life in harmony with your values is an important factor in personal happiness; you'll find that your life has much more clarity and makes more sense. Committing to and applying them causes you to take on new energy and freshness, which open up the potential for success, achievement, and personal fulfillment.

Ben Franklin devised a fine plan to mold his character. He was in his twenties when he worked it out, and he was still using it well into his late seventies. It was simple. He created a list of eight values, choosing them for their practicality in helping him mold his character, enhance his public image, make a good impression on others, and get ahead in the world. Once he had his values in place, he wrote them in a notebook. Each week he'd work on a single value for the entire week. The next week he'd work on another, until he completed his list, and then he'd begin all over again. At the end of each day he'd record his successes and failures in maintaining that day's value. In his old age, he said that this method made him a better and happier man. Franklin took his values seriously, so seriously that when a friend told him he was overly prideful Franklin took that to heart and added another value to his list: humility.

Gandhi honored truth and passive nonresistance as his core values, and when he was called upon to uphold them he did so with amazing courage and inordinate strength. Though he was a man of slight build and humble in appearance, he managed singlehandedly to bring the British Empire to its knees. He did this by sticking to his values, even when his supporters encouraged him to take more direct action.

Values reflect what you stand for and what you hold to be significant. They indicate what you should do; they also dictate what you should not do. Although this book is not about the business world, personal values have a great deal to do with personal ethics and how people function in the world of business. It's much easier to make ethical decisions when you are living by your own personal values than by trying to emulate someone else's. Knowing what your own ethical base is can enlighten your decisions and make them much more forceful and powerful.

The number of values you can rack up is not as important as the clarity you bring to them. They should mirror your current reality, as well as help you envision what you can achieve in the future. A strong set of core values guides you toward living from the inside out, rather than living from the outside in.

WHAT MAKES YOU YOU?

The first—and for many the most important—step you can take in understanding your soul's spiritual DNA is to identify what you value. This section leads you through some processes to help you choose, define, and prioritize just what it is that you hold true in your life.

Discerning your values is interior work; this means it's very private stuff. You may want to share your values with others or ask for their assistance at a later time, but not right now. This is a time for you to be with you, with your inner self, connecting with your soul. This process can rarely be done quickly. What's the rush, anyway?

Take time to be reasonable and honest with yourself. It might take a while to sort through the "shoulds," "coulds," and "ought tos" before you get to your basic core beliefs and principles. *Don't quit.* Even if the process takes you some time, don't give up on it. Keep on plugging away at it.

Getting Ready

First, choose a good place to do this work. Maybe propped up in bed, or soaking in the tub (bathtub, hot tub, Jacuzzi), or sitting in a park or a garden, or walking along a quiet pathway, or watching the waves crash along a beach, or . . . you'll know. When you choose the right place, stick to it if you can.

Let's start. There are three steps to answering "What's important to me?":

1. Identify your values

2. Define them carefully

3. Prioritize them wisely

Step One: Identify Your Values

As you go through this process, ask yourself, *Is this a* must *(internal) value for me?* You want to identify only those values that will be the cornerstone of your life. You want to eliminate any "should" values that are simply means to an end. We offer four approaches: (1) intuitional, (2) tried-and-true Q&A, (3) word-evaluation, and (4) jumpstart. Choose the approach that best fits you.

Intuitional Approach

In the intuitional approach, you place absolute trust in your own intuition. You trust that a sense of what you value will well up from your inner being. You are comfortable with it, you welcome it, and you wait upon it. You realize that your responses are not knee jerk or right off the top of your head. Here are two suggestions for how to begin.

First, look at your calendar, appointment book, organizer, check book, and so on. Where have you been spending your resources (time is a resource) this week, this month, this year? Do you see any patterns? If so, write them down. Are there key words that describe the patterns? Write them down. Now circle these key words; they are your preliminary values. (Positive key words might be *benevolence*, *kindness*, and so forth.) List your keywords separately.

The second suggestion is, with your journal or a pad of paper in front of you, to sit quietly and let Spirit speak through you and then write down those values (qualities, ideas, beliefs) that arise spontaneously from within. List as many as you can. (The values list at the end of this chapter may be helpful.) Then circle these potential values and write them on a separate sheet of paper in preparation for Step Two.

Tried-and-True Q&A Approach

Choose five or more from the questions that follow. Write down your answers as completely as you can. Since these are intended to be thought provokers, you might want to take a few days thinking about them before formulating your answers.

- How would you define your fundamental character?

- What brings real meaning to your life?

- What is so important to you that you wouldn't change it under any circumstances?

- What are the five factors that influence decisions you make?

- What positive words describe how you got to where you are now in life?

- What are the best things that have ever happened to you?

- What experiences have you had out of which you gained clarity about something in your life?

- What is your most important relationship?

- When you talk with others about what's important to you, what do you say?

- What *is* important to you? What are your passions or interests?

- What do you stand for?

- What aspect of your life would you like to change, enhance, or clarify?

Now look over your responses and underline or circle the word or words that are most important to you. List as many of them as you can. Write them down on a separate sheet of paper in preparation for Step Two.

Word-Evaluation Approach

Look over the chart called "Identify Your Core Values" at the end of this chapter. The choice of words in this list is based on many years of experience working with individuals and groups in discerning core values. If there is a word you feel should be included, add it. Note the rating scale at the top of the chart, and place the appropriate number next to each word. List your "very important for me" words on a separate sheet of paper.

Your core values will emerge from the "very important for me" category, but the other two categories contain valuable information for you as well. At some point, look especially at the "not important" category, and ask yourself, "Why do I reject that value? Why has it so little meaning for me?"

This process may be time-consuming, but you'll gain a complete sense of what you do and don't value.

Jump-Start Approach

If you want to speed up the process, scan the list of core values in the chart at the end of this chapter. Circle all those words that immediately call out to you "Circle me!" Then write the words on a separate sheet of paper.

Now, narrow it down. Whichever method you chose, you probably have lots of words listed. Recheck your list, and add or eliminate words. Cross out words that now appear similar. Words such as "friendship" and "belonging," on second glance, may be essentially the same to you. Do any words come to mind now that escaped your attention earlier? If so, add them to your list. If you have second thoughts about any word, then cross it out.

Study your list carefully, and circle *only* those words that represent values you want to uphold in your life. Circle as many as you like, but keep in mind that these are intended to be the key values by which you'll be living your life; therefore, the more words you choose the more likely you are to forget them. It's better to have three to five specific "I can do" values than a long laundry list of nice-sounding words.

Step Two: Define Your Values

Now that you have your essential list of values, define one by one, in sentence form, what each of these values means to you in the context of your own life. (You might want to go back and narrow down your list once more.) For example, if you have chosen the value "compassion," you might write:

Compassion. A feeling that comes over me when I see others in pain. A feeling of caring for others that is nonjudgmental. A consciousness of the challenges others face and a selfless tenderness towards them.

This may take you a while, but keep at it. We have found this to be a valuable exercise in clarifying what it is you believe in. Keep defining and refining in writing. Nothing makes a point clearer than writing it out.

Step Three: Prioritize Your Values

You've chosen your values, and you've defined them. The next step is to prioritize them, in order from highest to lowest. Does this mean that one value is "better" than another or that one is the "best" of them all? Not at all. It is simply a way for you to more fully understand what your own priorities are. If values are so important in our lives, then it's good to know which values predominate.

Let's use an example you may be familiar with. Centuries ago, in his letter to the spiritual community at Corinth (1 Corinthians 13), Paul of Tarsus gave us an excellent core value process. In this instance, he was discussing love.

Paul first identified the importance of love, "What if I could speak all languages of humans and of angels? If I did not love others, I would be nothing more than a noisy gong or a clanging cymbal."

Then he defined what it is, "Love is kind and patient, never jealous, boastful, proud, or rude. Love isn't selfish or quick-tempered. It doesn't keep a record of wrongs that others do. Love rejoices in the truth, but not in evil. Love is always supportive, loyal, hopeful, and trusting. Love never fails!"

Finally, he prioritized it, "For now there is faith, hope, and love. But of these three, the greatest is love." This is an example of high-level clarity.

Unlike Paul, however, some people just don't like the whole idea of ranking. What then?

Ken Wilber, in his book *One Taste*, answers the objection, "If you don't like values ranking and want to avoid them, then fine, that is your value ranking—you rank nonranking as better than ranking—and that itself is a ranking, *your* ranking. . . . The fact is, ranking is unavoidable in values, so at least do it consciously, honestly, and above board."

The priority you put on one value over another may vary with time and circumstances, but your values will probably remain with you for the rest of your life.

VALUES WORKSHEET

Now create a worksheet of your values in priority and defined order. Keep this list; you'll need it when you begin working on your purpose statement in Chapter Four, and again when you create your Life Map in Chapter Ten.

Here's an example of how to elaborate on your top values. This is a good place to do this work so your values and definitions will be at hand as you continue using this book.

(EXAMPLE)
Value: *Compassion*
Definition: *A feeling that comes over me when I see others in pain. A feeling of caring for others that is nonjudgmental. A consciousness of the challenges others face and a selfless tenderness towards them.*

1. Value: _____
   Definition: _____
2. Value: _____
   Definition: _____
3. Value: _____
   Definition: _____
4. Value: _____
   Definition: _____
5. Value: _____
   Definition: _____

IDENTIFY YOUR CORE VALUES

Use this list to help you identify what your core values might be, or develop a list of your own. To use this list as a way to determine your priorities, we suggest applying a rating scale, placing the appropriate number next to each word:

> 3 = very important for me
> 2 = important for me
> 1 = not so important for me

___ Acceptance	___ Charity	___ Effectiveness
___ Accountability	___ Comfort	___ Efficiency
___ Accuracy	___ Commitment	___ Equality
___ Achievement	___ Communication	___ Ethics
___ Adaptability	___ Community	___ Excellence
___ Advancement	___ Compassion	___ Excitement
___ Adventure	___ Competence	___ Expertise
___ Aesthetics	___ Conservativeness	___ Faith
___ Affection	___ Consistency	___ Faithfulness
___ Ambition	___ Contribution	___ Fame
___ Analytical	___ Cooperation	___ Family
approach	___ Courtesy	___ Femininity
___ Assertiveness	___ Creativity	___ Finances
___ Attentiveness	___ Culture	___ Financial
___ Attractiveness	___ Decisiveness	security
___ Authority	___ Democracy	___ Fitness
___ Autonomy	___ Dependability	___ Flair
___ Beauty	___ Discipline	___ Flexibility
___ Calmness	___ Diversity	___ Forgiveness
___ Caring	___ Duty	___ Freedom
___ Challenge	___ Ecology	___ Friendship
___ Change	___ Education	___ Frugality

___ Fun	___ Maturity	___ Recognition
___ Generosity	___ Meaningfulness	___ Reliability
___ Genuineness	___ Merit	___ Religion
___ Gratitude	___ Mindfulness	___ Reputation
___ Growth	___ Moderation	___ Resourcefulness
___ Health	___ Modesty	___ Respect
___ Helping	___ Money	___ Responsibility
___ Honesty	___ Nature	___ Responsiveness
___ Honor	___ Nonconformity	___ Results
___ Hope	___ Nurturance	orientation
___ Humor	___ Openness	___ Risk taking
___ Independence	___ Order	___ Romance
___ Industriousness	___ Passion	___ Safety
___ Imagination	___ Peace	___ Security
___ Inner harmony	___ Perfection	___ Self-acceptance
___ Innovation	___ Perseverance	___ Self-control
___ Integrity	___ Personal	___ Self-esteem
___ Intellectual	development	___ Self-knowledge
status	___ Personal growth	___ Self-reliance
___ Intimacy	___ Pleasure	___ Self-respect
___ Inventiveness	___ Popularity	___ Self-sufficiency
___ Involvement	___ Positive attitude	___ Serenity
___ Joy	___ Possessions	___ Service
___ Justice	___ Power	___ Sexuality
___ Kindness	___ Practicality	___ Simplicity
___ Knowledge	___ Preservation	___ Skills
___ Leadership	___ Privacy	___ Solitude
___ Learning	___ Productivity	___ Sophistication
___ Leisure	___ Professionalism	___ Spirituality
___ Love	___ Progress	___ Stability
___ Loyalty	___ Purity	___ Status
___ Masculinity	___ Purpose	___ Success
___ Mastery	___ Quiet	___ Teamwork

___ Time   ___ Trust   ___ Wisdom

___ Tolerance   ___ Truth   ___ Wittiness

___ Toughness   ___ Variety   ___ Work

___ Tradition   ___ Versatility

___ Tranquillity   ___ Wealth

4

Why Are You Here?

Finding Your Unique Life's Purpose

Purpose serves as a principle around which to organize our lives.
ANONYMOUS

At some point in your life, you've asked yourself, *What am I really here for?* Way down deep in your innermost being, you've had the feeling that you're here to do something, and your inner self is giving you little nudges of discontent, even when everything appears to be working for you. This inner hint is reminding you that you have a unique purpose for being, and that you really ought to take time to look into it!

You have a unique role to play on this planet. Conscious of it or not, you have a purpose or a mission in life just waiting to be fulfilled, and only you can do it. This is a "call" from God to express your unique individuality, to embody a sense of wholeness, to be in the world in a way that reflects who you truly are. It is your essence. As psychologist Abraham Maslow observed, "We all need something bigger than we are to be awed by and to commit ourselves to."

One night, Dan Rather of "CBS Evening News" reported the amazing story of Chris Gardner, an African American who is "living large" by living into his purpose. Today, Gardner is a high-level stockbroker with all the perks of a successful career, including beautiful homes, cars, clothes. But that's not the life Gardner always had. Only a few years ago, he was a divorced homeless man with custody of his small son. He called a public restroom in a subway station in

Oakland, California, home. He knew in his heart, however, that God had a higher purpose for him. The first step for him was to find his way to San Francisco's Glide Memorial Church. There he found food and shelter for himself and his son, but more important he found people who shared his vision that life can be lived with dignity and without fear. Each morning, Chris Gardner walked out the door of the church shelter and in through the doors of the major financial institutions in the city. The brokerage house of Dean Witter decided to take a chance on this homeless high school dropout, and their willingness to invest in him paid off. Gardner became one of the firm's most creative and productive financial analysts. Today he heads his own investment firm in Chicago and is a respected leader in the field. Just as powerful is his recommendation to others. He advises that living into your purpose cannot be separated from serving others. Sound familiar? Isn't that another way of saying "love your neighbor as yourself"?

FINDING YOUR PURPOSE

So what, and where, is your purpose in life? Why hasn't it shown up yet? That's the challenge. Unless you've had a revelation, a personal epiphany—you know, the heavens open up, celestial trumpets blast, and a shining angel declares your purpose—you'll need to go through a discovery process.

Your purpose isn't visible to the naked eye because it's encoded and embedded deeply within you, and it requires your discernment to discover or uncover it. It's bundled with your values and your vision in what we call the nucleus of your spiritual DNA; it's your "imprisoned splendor" waiting to come forth. It's as individual and unique to you as it is to every other person on this planet. It's a golden key waiting for you to unlock a whole new perspective for your life.

What might prevent you from embarking on this quest? Stephen Covey, in *First Things First,* says there is a huge distinction between what actually is important and what is urgent. Do you fill your to-do list only with activities that reflect your life's purpose? Indeed, are you convinced you have a life purpose and understand what it is? In the movie *Mr. Holland's Opus*, the hero is a high school music teacher who considers his teaching post as little more than a way to make money. His real life's work is composing his great musical work, his opus. Holland lives through more than thirty boring years of teaching music, without finishing his opus, until one day he comes to a life-changing realization that he's actually been working on his opus: not by putting notes on paper, but as a composer of hopes and dreams in the contributions he's made to the lives of so many students over so many years. When this sinks in, he has an incredible sense of personal satisfaction and realizes that, unknowingly, he's been working at his life's purpose for years.

YOU CAN MAKE A DIFFERENCE

Let's consider two real people who made a decided difference in the history of the United States: Paul Revere, whose name is well known, and a blacksmith whose name isn't. Each had his part to play.

Revere was a successful businessman, a well-known silversmith, who had an intense desire to do something more compelling than his occupation. He joined the cause for the independence of the American colonies from England. On the night of April 18, 1775, he was given an assignment to watch for a prearranged light signal from the tower of the Old North Church in Boston: two lights if the British were coming by ship, one light if by land. When he saw the signal, he was to travel by horseback as fast as he could to warn the colonists in Lexington. Around midnight the signal was given: two lights appeared in the tower. Revere jumped on his borrowed horse and rode at breakneck speed on the long journey to warn the colonials that "The British are coming!"

The ride and rider became immortalized in Henry Wadsworth Longfellow's poem "The Midnight Ride of Paul Revere." But there were two people, remember? Revere and a blacksmith. History has given Revere the lion's share of the credit. It has a tendency to do that with headliners. It has not given us the blacksmith's name, though legend has called him "Jonathan." He played an equal role in that historic midnight ride. There is another old fable you might recall:

> For want of the nail, the shoe was lost,
> For want of the shoe, the horse was lost,
> For want of the horse, the rider was lost,
> For want of the rider, the battle was lost,
> For want of the battle, the kingdom was lost.
> All for the want of a nail.

Paul Revere's purpose that night in 1775 was to spread the alarm, but to do so he was reliant on the ability of his horse, since without the speed of the horse the battle could have been lost. As Longfellow wrote: "The fate of a nation was riding that night." "Jonathan" too had a clear purpose in life: to make people's lives better by taking proper care of their horses. Sounds like a rather mundane occupation, doesn't it? But consider that "Jonathan's" commitment to his purpose indirectly helped to create a new nation. If you can do one thing that positively affects another human being—or a nation of them—you have fulfilled your purpose.

CIRCUMSTANCES CHANGE, BUT YOUR PURPOSE REMAINS CONSTANT

Knowing your purpose can be a lifesaver. The one thing we can count on in life is change. Regardless of how well prepared you think you are, and when you least expect it, life is going to hit you with a few surprises. Some hits are minor, some are very dramatic. It's probably happened to you once or twice, or to someone you know. Think of the large number of people who felt quite secure about their investments up to September 10, 2001. They could tell you almost to the penny what their retirement income would be; their security was assured. But whose financial planning could have accounted for September 11? Within a short time, those once-secure investments failed, investment houses went belly-up, entire corporations folded in the aftermath, 401(k)s lost their value, and retired people were forced to look for work. Folks found that security is really illusory.

Regardless of the obstacles life may put in your way every now and then, understanding your purpose will center you and keep you centered in your true being, which is the real source of your power and security. You learn to rely on your own inner strength, not on people or things outside of your center. You no longer have to put yourself at the bidding of others because you are centered in yourself rather than self-centered; you are rooted and grounded in your true nature. As Minot Simons said, "No pleasure philosophy, no sensuality, nor place nor power, no material success can for a moment give such inner satisfaction as the sense of living for a good purpose."

YOUR PURPOSE IS NOT YOUR JOB

Many people define themselves by their careers, especially in North America. But your purpose for being is not about your job or career; nor is it intended to help you find "the right position" for you. It's vital, as you go through this process, to keep things in perspective. You are not your job, and your job is not you. Jobs can change; your reason for being does not change. Laurie Beth Jones says in *The Path*, "Once you know what you were put here to do, then a job is only a means towards your [purpose], not an end in itself."

The movie *Jerry Maguire* opens with Tom Cruise as Jerry, wrestling over a number of issues, including what has become of him. He senses that some of the predicaments he's let himself get caught up in truly offend his sense of values. So, using these values as a marker, he sits down and writes out a personal purpose statement that includes values such as "simple pleasures," "caring," and "being the me I always wanted to be." Jerry realizes he has forgotten about what is really important. Writing out his purpose statement gives him an opportunity to figure that out. Similarly, you need to decide what meaning you want to give to your life. Remember, your purpose is not tied to your job, nor is it tied to your finances; it's tied to who you are.

WHAT A DIFFERENCE A PURPOSE MAKES

Being aware of your purpose:

- Causes you to examine your innermost thoughts and feelings

- Helps you uncover your talents and contributions

- Reveals your very reason for existence

- Helps you focus on what you want to be, do, and have in life

- Provides the necessary drive to inspire you to face challenges, overcome obstacles, and receive more meaning from life

In the process, you discover your talents, your interests, and your deepest desires. You see your life from many perspectives, and you may be surprised at what you discover about yourself from this new viewpoint.

Your personal purpose statement is not something you can come up with in thirty minutes, or even overnight. It takes careful introspection and analysis of your thoughts, ideas, beliefs, and attitudes, but the end result is worth the time spent because you will use this statement as your life's central organizing principle. It becomes your own personal constitution about what matters most to you. Clarity about your purpose, coupled with your core values, furnishes a starting place for creating your Life Map.

WRITING OUT YOUR
PERSONAL PURPOSE STATEMENT

Consider your personal purpose as something to discover, rather than something to define. Think of it as a step-by-step guide to how you want to live your life. Creating your purpose statement gives you a deep and complete commitment to follow your innermost values. When faced with a difficult situation, you will have this statement to consult and assist you to make a choice that is in line with your values.

Yes, as busy as you are, you must commit your purpose to writing. This written document is a clear statement of what you do and why you do it. It includes the guiding principles you live by, and the rules you observe. It imparts overall direction for what you want to be. It can become a powerful voice to what's important, meaningful, and fun for you.

There's a practical side to it, too. Thoughts seem to become untangled as they pass from your lips to your fingertips. If you can say it and write it, you have thought it through clearly.

Should a Purpose Statement Be Short?

This is your statement. You can make it long, involved, and complicated, if you wish. But what's the point? Powerful and meaningful statements don't need to be long; nor do they need flowery language. Laurie Beth Jones puts it succinctly in *The Path*. She says that a purpose statement should be:

- No more than a single sentence

- Easily understood by a twelve-year-old

- Easy to recite from memory at gunpoint

She doesn't literally mean someone will put a gun to your head. She's saying that your statement should be so firmly fixed in your consciousness that you can easily recite it even under trying circumstances. Your purpose statement should be concise, creative, descriptive, believable, understandable, motivating, achievable . . . and *short*.

The Process

Some people can dive right in and write draft after draft on a yellow pad until their statement is crystal clear. If you're not like that, and need some support, here are a few hints:

- Your written statement shouldn't be a catch-all. Management guru Peter Drucker says that one of the most common mistakes people make is to turn their thoughts "into a kind of hero sandwich of good intentions," where everything is thrown in. He recommends, "Say what you mean, and say it in standard language." When you decide to share it with others, it won't be necessary for them to admire the beauty of the language, but they must be able to understand it.

- Write in a format that's comfortable for you. For example, you might want to write in a flowing stream of consciousness and forget the rules of grammar, for now. Or you could write your thoughts in short topical paragraphs on five-by-eight cards and then arrange them in logical order. Or you could write in clipped phrases using a bulleted list. Or you could set up a flipchart, get out the markers, and create a pie chart. Some people like to stick large sheets of paper on the wall with a topic heading on each sheet and then jot down ideas as they arise. You'll find the best format for you.

- It's often easier to write about someone else or something else than to write about yourself. You may find it difficult at first to write succinctly about you. There are times when it's easier to write a whole page than one really clear, concise sentence, so this may not be an instant process.

- Don't let grammar, spelling, sentence structure, or style inter- fere. This is not intended to be a piece of creative writing. Write what you sense to be true about the way you want to live, rather than how you are living now.

- This is for your eyes only (unless you choose to show it to others).

- Keep this question in mind as you write down each thought, "Does this inspire the best in me?"

- Some people enjoy asking others to evaluate what they have written, and they value their input. However, if you use expressive language in your draft to help make a point to yourself, you might consider doing some editing before you let someone else read it.

- If you know what you want to say but can't get it down on paper, try dictating your thoughts onto a tape recorder, transcribing them to paper, and only afterward putting them in some sort of order.

- You may prefer to verbalize aloud your life's purpose, or talk about it with a trusted friend, and then write down some notes on what you have said.

Whichever method you choose, hang in there. Stay with it until you are completely satisfied. It's unlikely you will thoroughly clar- ify and narrow your purpose statement until at least several drafts have been written. Here's a maxim to keep in mind, "There's no good writing, only good rewriting," or, as some might feel, "I hate writing. I love having written."

Life Map Notes: Discovering Your Purpose

Now you are ready to begin working on your purpose statement. This exercise gives you an opportunity to think about your life and how you are living it. The objective is to make your core values and your purpose a part of you.

Set ground rules before you begin. Some prefer to be in silence during this process, while others work best surrounded by stimuli. Determine how you work best, and what your personal ground rules are. If you like solitude, what does that mean, and how do you carry it out? Where? Should the phone be on or off? the TV? the stereo? What about the kids? What about pets? Will you be off-limits during your process times?

In the accompanying text, we offer two methods to create your purpose. The first is a four-step, quite thorough process, and the second is more open-ended, a Q&A approach. Choose the one that suits you and your style. When you're ready, begin.

Step One: Discern

Answer as completely as you can these three questions, which are the key components that make up a purpose statement. Write as completely as you can. Write as much as you need. Purpose statements contain strong, active verbs, such as *grow, serve, transform, change, manifest, express*.

1. Who are you?

Hint: Keep in mind that you are a spiritual being having a human experience, and that your true identity is an expression of the sacred.

_____

_____

2. What do you want to accomplish?

Hint: This refers to what you want to manifest in your life. It might be those hidden glimpses of potential waiting to be drawn out. Or your response might be to state your goals clearly.

_____

_____

3. How you will do this?

Hint: This refers to the pathways, the means, you use to bring out your potential and realize your goals.

_____

_____

Step Two: Summarize

Once you've answered all three questions to your satisfaction, summarize your responses, one question at a time. You'll end up with three separate statements. Examples:

I am a child of God. I have been abundantly blessed with many, many gifts in my life. The greatest gift is the love which I know God has for me.

I believe that God is calling me to bring into being God's great love, not only in my own life, but also to see it reflected in the lives of those around me.

I can accomplish this purpose by active service to others in such a way that I am benefited even more than those whom I may serve.

If you feel "complete" about your summarization, skip steps three and four.

_____

_____

_____

_____

Step Three: Compose

Compose those sentences into a single paragraph that clearly conveys what you are about. An example:

> I am a child of God. I have been blessed with many gifts, the greatest of which is God's love for me. I believe I'm called to manifest God's love in my life and to see it in the lives of others. I can do this through service to others, which really benefits me more than those whom I serve.

_____

_____

_____

_____

Step Four: Condense and Finalize

Keep the essence of the paragraph, but remove all extraneous words and phrases so you end up with one single sentence. Example:

> I am a blessed child of God called to express God's love by serving others and experiencing that love through service.

_____

_____

_____

_____

Alternative Approach: Open-Ended Q&A

Here's a paradox: life is not about asking and answering questions, it's about making decisions. But we often need to ask and answer questions before we can make reasonable and right decisions. In this approach, you first write down your initial responses to the direct questions given here, and then you follow the earlier process. Use as many of the questions as you would like. Use them as is or rewrite them to make them more applicable to you. The point is to trigger a response.

- What am I really good at?

- What do I really enjoy?

- What do I enjoy doing most?

- What am I doing that is not very productive?
  Why do I keep doing it?

- What are my greatest strengths?

- What strengths have those who know me noticed in me?

- If I had unlimited time and money, what would I do?

- When I look at my work life, what activities do I
  consider of greatest worth?

- What have been my happiest moments in life? Why?

- When I look at my personal life, what activities do I
  consider of greatest worth?

- What are my important roles in life?

- What are the most important lifetime goals I want to
  fulfill in each role?

- What results am I currently getting in my life that I don't like?

- What would I really like to do in my life?

_____

_____

_____

_____

_____

_____

_____

_____

5

Where Do You Want to Go in Your Life?

Creating Your Vision for the Future

*Far away in the sunshine are my highest aspirations. I look up and
see the beauty, believe in them and try to follow where they lead.*
LOUISA MAY ALCOTT

Florence, Italy, is a city of marvelous works of art. Three of the
most visited masterpieces are Botticelli's "Birth of Venus" in
the Uffizi Gallery, the great bronze doors by Ghiberti in the bap-
tistry of the Duomo, and Michelangelo's sculpture "David," which
stands at the end of a long corridor in the Galleria dell'Accademia.
The monumental sculpture is the result of Michelangelo's vision of
the young lad featured in the biblical story of David and Goliath.

You probably know the story of the villagers who were terror-
ized by Goliath, a gargantuan man, taller and stronger than anyone,
who used his strength to subjugate everyone. No one knew how to
bring the bully down, or if they did have an idea, no one was brave
enough to carry it out. So the people lived in great fear, unable to
determine their own destiny. Then appears young David, a shep-
herd boy on the verge of manhood, who is gutsy enough to say that
he could topple Goliath with one deft blow of his slingshot.
Michelangelo portrayed him as he might have looked at a specific
moment before the fight, with his slingshot thrown over his left
shoulder, standing tall and focused on his task. He's been standing
there poised for the fight since 1504.

When you gaze upon the beauty of the figure, what you see is the
end result of a dream in the mind of Michelangelo made palpable.

Long before Michelangelo ever picked up his chisel and began carving, he had a vision—his thoughts, impressions, and ideas of the figure imprisoned inside the rough marble block before him. The artist carefully chipped away at the block to release his vision within. It stands today, some five hundred years later, as a visible testimony of one man's compelling vision. We don't know what form another sculptor might have released from the same stone. We do know that the sculpture that emerged was born of Michelangelo's vision: a composite of all his thoughts, feelings, impressions, and ideas.

A CLEAR VISION

Everyone has visions and dreams. What is your dream, your vision, your picture, for the future? What lies within you waiting to be released?

The fact is, many people do not have a clear vision of where they want to be in the future. As psychologist Linda Phillips-Jones writes in *Creating or Revising Your Personal Vision*, "If you don't identify your vision others will plan and direct your life for you. I've worked with too many individuals who late in their lives said, 'If only. . . .' You don't have to be one of them." Someone else's picture of what your life should be is not your vision, any more than your picture of their future is their vision.

Alice, in Lewis Carroll's *Alice in Wonderland*, was one of those "if only" people. Alice was lost. When she came across a Cheshire Cat in a tree, she wondered if the Cat would help her find her way:

> "Would you tell me, please, which way I ought to go from here?"
>
> "That depends a good deal on where you want to get to," said the Cat.
>
> "I don't much care where—" said Alice.
>
> "Then it doesn't matter which way you go," said the Cat.

"—so long as I get somewhere," Alice added as an explanation.

"Oh, you're sure to do that," said the Cat, "if only you walk long enough."

The Cheshire Cat was saying to Alice, "I can't tell you what direction to take until you tell me where you are headed." Alice didn't seem to care, and she was willing to go in any direction. Well, on the basis of that logic, she would certainly get somewhere—but it was unlikely to be where she really wanted to go.

Why wander aimlessly? A clear vision gets you from where you are now to where you want to be—not simply somewhere, or "anywhere but here," but to a specific predetermined destination. As futurist Joel Barker says in *The Power of Vision*, "Vision without action is merely a dream. Action without vision just passes the time. Vision with action can change the world."

WHAT IS VISION?

The *Oxford English Dictionary* lists a number of meanings for vision: the act or faculty of seeing; a thing or person seen in a dream or trance; a thing or idea perceived vividly in the imagination; imaginative insight; statesmanlike foresight, sagacity in planning; a person [or thing] of unusual beauty; what is seen on the television screen. That's a lot of ways to think about vision! Let's consider a few more.

When we speak of your vision, we are talking about those thoughts, ideas, and feelings that you really cherish and that capture your heart and mind in such a compelling way that you are willing to commit your resources of time, talent, and treasure to make your vision a reality.

A vision can be a desired future you don't now have, or it can be a mental image of what is now and how it could improve. It's like an ever-evolving mosaic of pictures that will successfully implement your purpose. It focuses on what you want to accomplish within the boundaries set by your values and your purpose. This lays responsibility on you because you do not want anything in your future that violates your personal values, or that is not in complete harmony with your purpose for being.

Your vision as a positive picture of your desired future must be realistic, believable, and attractive. It is a dream in action, a launching pad for the future.

It's a snapshot of what you want to be, do, feel, own in the future; a mental picture of what could or what should be; a visual reality that exists at an internalized and personal level.

A vision is an image of your inner values, feelings, and beliefs. It is what you see when you carry out your purpose.

Vision requires stretching reality beyond the present by looking and thinking ahead. It does not fixate on the present; nor does it attempt to replay the past. Not every vision culminates in success, but without vision no success is possible, so never dismiss your visionary thoughts as pipe-dream fantasies. Visions are a spark of life that can help you feel motivated, awakened, hopeful, and enthusiastic. Visions encourage you to grow, develop, and create.

Your vision is unique to you. It is what you want for yourself and your world around you. As an individual, each person's vision is just that: personal! What you dream for you is surely different from what your neighbor or colleague envisions. It might even be different from what your spouse envisions. Vision keeps you moving forward, even against discouraging odds. As you work at creating your vision, be daring and reach for what you truly want for yourself.

Lance Armstrong has long held bodily strength and endurance as personal values that define optimal health. As an outstanding competitive cyclist, these values were important in his vision of being able to compete in and win the famed Tour de France race. They continued to be important even after he learned that he had testicular cancer. But rather than trading in his values and giving up on his dream, he decided to go forward. Armstrong has now won five Tours de France and continues to compete; he knows that not even a serious disease has the power to diminish a personal vision.

VISION IN A NUTSHELL

Vision can be summarized by these seven characteristics:

1. Vision encompasses your whole being: heart, mind, soul, strength.

2. Vision taps into deeply rooted cares and concerns.

3. Vision helps you to assert what you want to create and attain.

4. Vision is what change and transformation might look like.

5. Vision allows you to reach for your highest potential.

6. Vision has no deadlines, no "by when's."

7. Vision is flexible and always subject to change and expansion.

VISION AND PURPOSE
ARE NOT THE SAME

Some say vision and purpose are interchangeable. We politely disagree. Vision and purpose both reflect core values, but they are *not* the same and they are *not interchangeable*. Core values are a precise definition of what you stand for. Your purpose statement is crafted to define precisely what your reason for being is, what you are called to do.

Your core values and your purpose both remain constant, providing the foundation for your vision, which can—and must— change. This is an important concept to keep in mind.

THE PARADOX OF VISION

Vision helps us see beyond the present by furnishing a clear picture of a new future reality and what it would look like. The paradox is that though vision draws you toward the future, its unfolding is experienced in the present. Vision can be very real in the dream state. Take the example of Walt Disney. Soon after the completion of Disney World, *Hard News Cafe* reported that someone said to Mike Vance, creative director for Disney Studios, "Isn't it too bad Walt Disney didn't live to see this?" Mike replied, "He did see it—that's why it's here."

VISION AND PERSONAL CHOICE

Your image of your future can include your expectation of what might be, your fears of what might actually take place, and your dreams of what you want to happen.

According to Vaclav Havel, the first president of the Czech Republic, "Consciousness precedes reality, and not the other way around." Being intentional about the choices you make is important in creating your personal future. You don't exist in a vacuum; what you choose affects not only you but others as well. You may not like that burden, but it's there. For example, although you have almost unlimited options and choices before you, your choices affect others, and you are responsible not only for your choices but for consequences that may arise. It's like the old saying, "Be careful for what you ask for; you might just get it." Does this mean that the safest choice is to do nothing?

There's a Russian fable about an old peasant couple, Natasha and Ivan. Natasha was filled with fears and racked by indecision, and she didn't want to think about tomorrow. Everything frightened her. Ivan would say, "You must get out of the house; it isn't healthy staying cooped up in here." But Natasha would reply, "Oh, Ivan, I'm afraid to go outside; something might happen, and then what would

I do?" Eventually, Natasha became so scared that she spent all her time in one tiny room. Ivan despaired. One day, he dug a deep hole, built a big pine box, and put Natasha in it. Then he lowered the box into the ground. Natasha cried out: "Ivan, I'm so scared, it's dark in here." Ivan said, "Don't worry, in a little while you'll be in heaven." "Ivan, let me out!" Natasha yelled. "Why?" he asked. "Don't you want to go to heaven?" "I do," she said, "but heaven must be filled with strangers, and then what would I do?"

Your personal vision helps you overcome uncertainty. It brings you inspiration, clarity, a new sense of direction, and focus. It allows you to develop a deep understanding of yourself and how you relate to your world. It helps you live and work with intention, integrity, and authenticity. It guides you as you make conscious choices that strengthen your interconnectedness to others and assists you to recognize opportunities that propel you toward reaching your full potential.

WHOSE VISION IS IT, ANYWAY?

As you work to discern your vision, keep in mind that it is God's vision for you that you seek, "I reveal myself to them in visions, I speak to them in dreams" (Numbers 12:5–6). We believe that God speaks to us, and that each of us perceives God's voice differently. Some hear it as an interior voice speaking to them, others feel it in a persistent hunch or gentle nudge. What you are seeking is what God already has in mind for you.

Vision begins, then, with your spirituality, not with your work, and it is from this spiritual encounter with God that you see the possibilities to which God is calling you.

DREAMING THE POSSIBLE DREAM

Dreaming can be fun, and it's free. You can kick back, relax, pour yourself a tall one, and muse about what might be—everything from the mundane to the sublime to the ridiculous:

- How will the room look once it's rearranged?

- What is it like strolling down a wide boulevard in a foreign city?

- Can I envision myself in action at the board meeting of a major corporation?

- Can I see myself accepting a Nobel Prize?

- Shall I picture my ideal customized and accessorized car?

- What if I get into the headlines for some heroic deed?

- Shall I take my family on a world-class vacation trip?

- What about being a guest on *Emeril Live!* or appearing on *Jacques and Julia,* and preparing my specialty for an adoring TV audience?

- Can I see myself sitting in my own skybox at a sporting event?

- Would I like to help a little kid learn to read?

Dreaming is wonderful and can be fertile ground for visioning, but it's useless unless you move from the dream state to a reality that is rooted and grounded in substance. Henry David Thoreau wrote, "Build your castles in the air; that is where they should be. Now put the foundations under them." Let the "castles" be your hopes and dreams and visions for the future; let your values and your purpose be the solid foundation.

If you've ever observed a construction site over time, you know how long it takes to excavate the site, install the supporting girders, build wooden molds for the concrete, pour the concrete, let it dry, and remove the wooden molds before any further work can be done. It appears that it takes longer to build a strong foundation (which very few people will ever see) than to erect the building itself. But the strength of the foundation, and the care put into building it, is always reflected in the finished structure. Imagine two houses, one built on sand and the other on solid rock. The waters come and easily erode the base of the house that is built on sand, washing it away. The house that is built on solid rock . . . well, you get the point.

Creating your personal vision allows you the opportunity to reflect on who you are, examine what you're called to do, question your worldview, and get in touch with aspects of your life you might be (habitually?) overlooking. This process offers you a choice to change what you are dissatisfied with; be more open to the possibilities available to you by accessing your own creativity; and, by using your intelligence, determination, courage, and wisdom, be all that you can be.

DREAMS CAN, AND DO, COME TRUE

Our favorite vision story has been retold in a variety of ways, but it incorporates on a personal level the points we have just discussed. It's about Monty Roberts, who was the son of an itinerant ranch hand. His family frequently moved from one place to another, and young Monty's education was affected as he transferred from school to school. When Monty was in high school, the class was assigned an essay about what each youngster wanted to do when he or she grew up. (Remember those essays?) Anyway, Monty loved the assignment because it gave him a way to express his dream, his vision, of the future. He wrote a detailed seven-page description of what he'd like to become: a horse trainer, with a four-thousand-square-foot home, on his own two-hundred-acre ranch. Two days later, he handed in his paper. When he got it back, the teacher had written a large red F and a note, "See me after class."

Monty, of course, kept the appointment and asked, "Why did I get an F?" The teacher replied that the paper described an unrealistic vision, since he was a poor kid from an itinerant family with no financial resources. The teacher suggested that he go home and rewrite the paper in a way that reflected reality. A week later, after a great deal of soul searching, Monty Roberts went to the teacher, and handed in the same paper. He said, "You can keep the F, and I'll keep my dream."

Well, as radio commentator Paul Harvey often says, "And now for the rest of the story."

Today, Monty Roberts is a world-renowned rancher who often lectures about his innovative, gentle method of horse training. His home and his ranch are exactly as he envisioned them, and his remarkable life has been made into a movie you may have seen, *The Horse Whisperer*. Monty's teacher learned the power of a dream from his former student and now brings students to the ranch to hear Monty's thrilling story of success.

So, what's the practical application of this story for you? It's to keep your vision firmly before you, and don't give up on your dream. As the spiritual says, "Keep your eye on the prize, and hold on!"

 Life Map Notes: Creating Your Vision Statement

Your vision statement should:

- Be realistic, credible, well articulated, and easy to understand

- Be consistent with your values and your purpose

- Describe, by painting a word picture in the present tense, your ideal future

- Be responsive to change (you can always add new pictures or amend old ones)

Remember to set your ground rules before you begin (see Chapter Four).

Step One: Preparation

Have this on hand:

- Your core values and your purpose statement

- A stack of four-by-six file cards, your journal, or a pad of paper

- A large sheet of paper

To begin, create a time line on the large sheet of paper. On the left-hand side, write today's date. On the far right, set a date that's three, four, or five years into the future.

Step Two: Dream Boldly

Close your eyes, relax, and begin daydreaming about your future—but in the present tense, and *beginning from the end date*. Why go backwards in the dream process, from the end date to the present? Because if you start with the present you might get stuck in current realities and find it difficult to get past them. By starting at the end date, you have an opportunity to look into the future, to where you want to be, and then proceed back to the present. For example, see yourself living in your ideal environment, not just *wishing* you lived there—or having trouble figuring out where this place is! Don't rush the process; it can take a while to get going.

When you have your image, write a descriptive word picture of your dream on an index card. Be sure to include a few words about how you will carry out your purpose based on your core values. Now affix your completed cards to the time line. Move them around as necessary so they form a story.

Step Three: Narrow the Dream

Once your numerous cards are in place, narrow down the number of cards till you end up with a few attainable, realistic dreams.

Step Four: Create a Preliminary Vision Statement

Write your preliminary statement clearly and concisely. Use nouns and adjectives to express your vision. Write in the present tense, as though it has already been accomplished. Fill it with descriptive details that anchor it to reality.

Here is an example:

> I see myself as a successful entrepreneur. I've developed new learning products that serve my customer base of young people in junior and senior high school. These products empower the students to excel in reading skills. Because of the value these products have, I see my company growing by more than 10 percent in sales each year for the next three years. I'm truly grateful for this opportunity to serve others.

Alternative Q&A Approach

If you are having trouble with steps one and two, try the Q&A method to prime your dreaming pump. Choose several of the questions given here; answer them as completely as you can. The point is to trigger a response from you. Then write a vision statement based on your responses.

- What do I really enjoy doing?

- What do I want to do?

- What brings happiness and joy into my life?

- What is most meaningful for me?

- What do I care about most?

- What do I want to do?

- What would I like to do for my loved ones? for my community? for the world?

- What issues and causes do I most care about?

- What contribution would I like to make in the future?

- What do I do in an excellent way?

- What do I want to have?

- What do I value in my relationships with other people?

- If I won the lottery, what would I do with the money?

- Where would I like to be one month from now?
  three months from now? six months from now?

- Where do I see myself one year from now? two years
  from now? five years from now?

- What impact on the future would I like to make?

- What changes in my life do I envision?

Now go back and follow steps three and four in the process.

PART II

Understanding Your Soul Type

Assessments and Practices

You are what your deep driving desire is.
As your deep driving desire is, so is your will.
As your will is so is your deed.
As your deed is so is your destiny.
THE UPANISHADS

In Part Two we explore the four soul types; these chapters are the heart, soul, mind, and strength of this book. Spirituality and religion are about behavior, not theory. To consider love for God, neighbor, and self as an idea is an illusion. To seek God with all your heart, mind, soul, and strength is not simply an idea; it is a practice.

Jung once said that the "pattern of God exists in every [person] and that this pattern in the individual has at its disposal the greatest transforming energies of which life is capable." Your task is to find your particular pattern for your individual self; if you do, your life will be transformed.

We hope you read through all four chapters, because each of the four soul types has unique importance and its own practices.

■ ■ ■

But if you have an itch to zero in quickly on your own soul type, do this:

1. Read the brief profile at the beginning of each chapter, take the short assessment at the end of the chapter, and record your scores. The soul type assessment in which you score highest is your primary soul type.

2. Go back and read the chapter material for your soul type. When you are ready, open your journal or get out your notes and move on to Chapter Ten, "Constructing Your Life Map."

6

Heart-Centered Spirituality
The Practice of Gratitude

Gratitude is not only the greatest virtue,
it is the parent of all others.
CICERO

PROFILE OF THE HEART-CENTERED SOUL TYPE

You enjoy stories about how individual lives have been changed by gratitude. You see life as something to be gratefully experienced and embraced in the here and now. Being in touch with the heart, feelings, and emotions is important to you, not just to understand them cognitively but to use them as a way to make your life holier, more joyful, more filled with gratitude. Personal renewal or transformation is central to your spirituality. You hunger for God to live in your heart. This hunger may be fed by a personal transforming experience, even if the experience is challenging. You may respond to this experience with feelings of thankfulness, well-being, or joy.

Teacher Plans a Gift of Gratitude," proclaims the headline on a *Washington Times* article about Bonnie Dukes, a mother of three who shared her gratitude in an incredibly moving gesture.

Bonnie is a high school English teacher who had to return to a teaching career in the midst of a nasty divorce and custody fight over her young daughters. Her two main companions during this period were turmoil and loneliness, so she decided to return to the safety of her home town and teach at her old high school. There, as a student, she had discovered a great appreciation and love for literature from her English teacher, David Knight.

She had always felt a deep sense of gratitude to him for getting her excited about literature, so she was amazed and pleased to learn that a bright, athletic-looking student in her English literature class was Andrew Knight, son of her former teacher. She was also astounded to learn that although Andrew appeared to healthy, he'd had only one functioning kidney since birth, and it was functioning at only 65 percent of its capacity. To make it worse, Andrew contracted amoebic dysentery on a mission trip to Guatemala the summer before his senior year. He couldn't shake it, and, the doctors told his parents, the result was his kidney had slowed down to 20 percent capacity. If Andrew did not get a kidney transplant soon, he'd be in danger of dying.

The immediate members of the Knight family were not suitable donors, and they prayed "that God would provide." Incredibly, Bonnie Duke's sense of gratitude to her old teacher would save the life of his son. Despite all her own life changes and legal problems, she offered one of her kidneys to save Andrew's life. "He's not just somebody else," she said, "he's one of my students, a fantastic kid who has the rest of his life to live." She knew that she was putting her own health at risk. Dave Knight said he looked her straight in the eye and asked, "Bonnie, are you sure you want to do this?" She had made up her mind. Her twelve-year-old daughter, Tiffany, shared how proud she was to have a mom so brave. Bonnie said, "What I'm doing could affect my life, but I've lived a good life, a rewarding and fulfilling life, and I have no regrets." Bonnie Dukes is a clear demonstration of how powerful a virtue gratitude can be.

We witnessed a less dramatic but equally instructive form of gratitude one morning at a Starbucks in Merced, near Yosemite National Park, as we spent a few moments over coffee before beginning a workshop presentation. An elderly woman came in, leaning heavily on a cane with one hand, and clutching a doctor's prescription in her other hand. She had a look of quiet desperation about her. She needed her prescription filled, but she didn't have the money to pay for it. She went to the counter and explained her predicament to Juan, the young "barista" on duty. Juan instinctively knew what had to be done. After checking with the other staff, he reached into the tip box and gave her all the cash they had, which was more than enough to pay for her prescription. These staff members were high school and college-age young people who probably could have used the tip money themselves, but they understood that what had been left in gratitude can also be used in gratitude.

GRATITUDE

No matter how you say it or display it, gratitude is a potent way to grow spiritually. Our friend Jordan Paul, in his latest book, *Becoming Your Own Hero*, comments, "Everything that is satisfying flows naturally from an open heart."

A heart that feels closed or constricted can be awakened through the practice of gratitude, a method for spiritual growth that is enormous. It's been observed that if the only prayer you ever said in your life is "Thank you," that would be enough. Gratitude can and should be part of the fabric of your everyday life. When you focus on what you are grateful for, the natural result is that you end

up having more. By concentrating on finding good in each circum-
stance, you find that your life is suddenly filled with gratitude. Do
you see the blessings in everyday life? Are you grateful for every
breath you breathe? Every thought you think? Are you grateful for
the vehicle that gets you around each day? No, not your car, but
your living vehicle, your body! How often do you bless your body,
or thank God for giving it to you?

You live through 86,400 seconds each day. How often are you
grateful for even one of them? Gratitude takes nothing for granted.
If you are a grateful person, you know about God's goodness—not
on the word of someone else, not because it's something you have
learned, but because it's something you have experienced. It's not
about being selective, such as being thankful only for the good stuff;
it's showing equal thanks for everyday blessings, even the small
things that are often taken for granted.

Kurt Vonnegut, Jr., in *Timequake*, said that his uncle Alex rec-
ommended noticing little things, the "simple occasions, not great
victories: maybe drinking lemonade on a hot afternoon in the
shade, or smelling the aroma of a nearby bakery, or fishing and not
caring if we catch anything, or hearing somebody all alone playing
a piano really well in the house next door." Vonnegut encourages
us to verbalize these small moments by saying on those occasions,
"If this isn't nice, what is?"

You probably do express gratefulness at one time or other for
the obvious blessings: a new addition to the family, a best friend, a
great job, a new home, a new pet, a new car, a nifty wardrobe, a trip
to some great place, a pay raise.

But how often have you expressed gratitude for any of these
everyday gifts: computers, telephones, the Internet, electric lights,
air conditioning, paved roads, coffee shops, grocery stores, sunshine,
flowers and plants, hummingbirds, trees, beautiful sunsets, clouds,
and soft rain?

TIME OUT!

Try this activity:

1. On a sheet of paper, write down five things for which you are grateful.

2. Now write the names of five people for whom you are grateful.

3. List five circumstances in your life for which you are grateful.

Next to each listing, indicate in a word or two why you are grateful.

What do you learn about yourself from this simple activity?

THE GRATITUDE REVOLUTION

We heard the words "Thank you, God" many times at a church we visited. People were enthusiastically singing praise music punctuated by joyful expressions of thanksgiving. They were expressing one of the practices most modeled by Jesus, who often gave God thanks and praise. At a supper with his disciples in an upper room, Jesus took bread and wine, blessed them, and gave thanks for them. In one form or other, this gratitude drama has been celebrated by Christians for two thousand years, using the words of Jesus recorded in the New Testament as a formula for giving thanks and praise.

This act of gratitude, like so many others in sacred writings, underscores the importance of being thankful. Heart-centered soul types understand the truth that is being shared here, that God showers us with continuous blessings, and our response should be grateful acceptance for what we've received and for what we will receive.

Lew Smedes learned gratitude the hard way after recovering from a life-threatening illness, but once he got it gratitude was overpowering. It was ultimate joy, he said, better than winning the lottery, even better than sex! Gratitude, for him, became the most important virtue a human being can express.

David Steindl-Rast, a Benedictine monk, writes passionately about the "gratitude revolution." His words have inspired books, articles, and discussion groups that explain the attraction of so many people to this gentle revolution. Gratitude embodies a sense of thankfulness, regardless of appearances, in all circumstances and situations of life. He sees it as an essential practice to bring healing and peace into one's life, even in the darkest moments. Is it possible to be grateful in a fearful time, such as what the United States faced on September 11, 2001? Steindl-Rast says yes, and asks us to go beyond our fears to wake up to the senselessness of violence and fanatical hatred. He wrote in his "Beliefnet" column on the Internet, "We can show ourselves grateful for the wake-up call . . . [because] a danger recognized and faced is cut in half." This happens, he says, when all of life is seen as a blessed and holy gift for which gratefulness is the only appropriate response.

This recognition of life as a gift is not unique to our times; it's been present in all traditions for centuries. Who would not resonate to the words of the Qu'ran when it speaks of God, "who has made the night for you, that you may rest therein, and the day, as that which helps you to see" (40, 61, 64)? Who would not understand the Buddhist view that "the worthy person is grateful and mindful of benefits done to him"? Or the profundity of the Midrashic teaching "In pleasure or pain, give thanks" (*Mekilta to Exodus*, 20.20)?

Melodie Beattie echoes those ancient comments in *A Review of the Lessons of Love*, "Gratitude unlocks the fullness of life. It turns what we have into enough and more. It turns denial into acceptance, chaos to order, confusion to clarity. It can turn a stranger into a friend. Gratitude makes sense of our past, brings peace for today, and creates a new vision for tomorrow."

Anne Frank was extremely grateful for life. This young Jewish girl kept a diary of her hiding in Amsterdam during World War II. She recorded in great detail her feelings, hopes, and fears—and most important, her belief that in spite of all the cruelty she and her family were facing, and the hardships they were enduring, life is good, beautiful, and worthwhile.

Lutheran theologian Dietrich Bonhoeffer, a brilliant writer and teacher, returned to Nazi Germany from the safety of England to assume leadership of the Confessing Church, which stood in opposition to the tyranny of Hitler. Bonhoeffer encouraged his people to become more involved in the resistance movement, even if it meant risking their own lives to help Jews escape from Germany. He was arrested during the last year of the war, and in that time of captivity, he wrote about the goodness of God and of God's creation, expressing thanks in his final letters for the opportunities that life had given him. With true joy in his heart he wrote, "In ordinary life we hardly realize that we receive a great deal more than we give, and it is only with gratitude that life becomes rich." Bonhoeffer carried this same sense of profound gratefulness with him as he made the long walk from his cell to the place of execution.

More recently, twenty-seven-year-old Aron Ralston from Colorado, on a "bouldering" trip in Utah, was trapped in the depths of a canyon when a five-hundred-pound rock fell on his hand, pinning it down. For five days, he tried everything he could to free himself. But nothing worked, no one heard his calls, and his food and water rations were running out. Rescue appeared unlikely, and he knew that if he were to survive, he'd have to take drastic action to free himself. The only course open to him was to amputate his hand at the place where he was pinned by the rock. Using a dull knife—the only tool available—he performed a self-amputation. It took him over an hour to cut through the bones, but he did it, and he was free. He used his hiking shorts as a tourniquet and slowly and painfully made his way to the trailhead, where he came upon two hikers who immediately assisted him. Aron was taken to St. Mary's Hospital in Moab, Utah, where he received desperately needed medical attention.

The facts of his story are remarkable in themselves, but more remarkable is his attitude toward his experience. When he met with the media for the first time after his ordeal, he expressed profound gratitude! He was grateful for his rescuers, for the skills of the hospital staff, for his mom and dad, and for the thoughts and prayers of the thousands of people who had prayed for him. He noted that his rescue took place on May 1, the National Day of Prayer, and he commented that this life-changing experience was for him a real opportunity to draw upon his spiritual resources.

Ralston's story is a dramatic and excellent illustration that we are not always responsible for our life experiences, but we are responsible for *our experience* of life. He said many people have been lucky to get as much as they can out of life, and for him "There is so much more I want to accomplish." With such a positive "attitude of gratitude," Aron will, no doubt, do just that.

Not every worthy story makes national news. Tom Holmes is an unusual guy who does unusual things. He's the owner of a fast-food restaurant with thirty employees on his payroll. Holmes believes in gratitude, so each morning he makes a point of personally greeting each employee by saying, "Thanks for coming in today." At the end of the workday, no one gets past his office without hearing from him, "Thanks for your hard work today; it really meant a lot." Tom works in an industry with high turnover. Estimates are that among fast-food restaurants in general it is 250 percent. He's cut his to 80 percent. He knows he can't expect people to stay in a high-turnover industry if they don't feel valued and special. He's found simple ways to express his appreciation as part of an employer-employee gratitude program, called "Giving Thanks." As the owner he models the practice, so every payday he writes a personal note of thanks to each person and places it in the envelope with the paycheck. The employees also play their role. The restaurant has a "Thanks Trophy," and each week at a short ceremony over ice cream one employee receives the trophy for doing something out of the ordinary that week. The next week this same employee selects a coworker to be the recipient and relates to the others what that person did to merit the trophy. The employees love the whole concept.

Heart-centered types grow spiritually by incorporating gratitude into all aspects of their lives, the good and the difficult. They are adept at turning negative into positive. It's how they demonstrate the true nature of the heart. In the face of challenge, heart-centered types say, "Thank you, God, for healing this situation." They know that God is present in the shadows and in the light.

HEART-CENTERED ASSESSMENT

Are you are a heart-centered soul type? Take this short assessment to see. Read each statement, and rank it using this scale:

> 3 = very important for me
> 2 = important for me
> 1 = not so important for me

1. I think of God as a loving parent. _____

2. I prefer unwritten spontaneous prayers, meditation, and affirmations that come right from the heart. _____

3. Flexibility rather than sticking to a pattern can help me grow spiritually. _____

4. Sacred writings have a central place in my spiritual growth.

   _____

5. I prefer spiritual communities that help me live a holier, purer life. _____

6. Telling people about how God has changed my life is important to me. _____

7. I respond to messages, lectures, and talks that have the power to change my life. _____

8. I easily express my gratitude to God for all of my life experiences. _____

9. Truly spiritual people display joy in their lives. _____

10. The aim of life is to love God and be loved in return. _____

11. I like to read about people whose lives were changed through the power of gratitude. _____

12. The arts—music, drama, films, sculpture, painting—can be used as ways to express gratitude to God. _____

Add up the numeric value of your responses, and write your total here: _____

HEART-CENTERED GRATITUDE PRACTICES

1. Say Grace (the word is from the Latin root for thankful) before not only meals but all activities for which you are thankful.

2. Begin and maintain a gratitude journal to record what you are grateful for each day. An alternative is to create a gratitude list of everything for which you're grateful, and add to it each time you discover a new blessing.

3. Begin and end your day with a prayer or thought of thanksgiving.

4. Start expressing thankfulness by sharing a heartfelt compliment or sending a thank-you note to people.

5. Practice a "random act of kindness," with no expectation of reward.

6. Give away a possession to someone as a means of saying thank you for your abundance.

7. Join a discussion group or class that looks at the importance of practicing gratitude. This might include a group or a chat room on the Internet.

8. Find and use, or write and use, silent affirmations or short prayers of thanks throughout the day.

9. Read about the power of gratitude. There are many books, articles, and Web pages on this topic.

10. Find an activity that fills you with sheer joy, in which a sense of gratitude overwhelms your being. It might be cooking, gardening, listening to or creating music, and so on.

7

Soul-Centered Spirituality
The Practice of Contemplation

With an eye made quiet by the power of harmony,
and the deep power of joy, we see into the life of things.
WILLIAM WORDSWORTH

PROFILE OF THE SOUL-CENTERED SOUL TYPE

You believe the purpose of life is to achieve union with the sacred, and you prefer to listen to God rather than speak to God as your primary interaction with the divine. For you, the real world is the interior world. *Intuitive, introspective,* and *contemplative* are adjectives used to describe this form of spirituality. You see yourself on a mystical journey into the holy, and you value opportunities to pause on the journey for quiet renewal of the spirit. This might happen on a retreat, or in daily meditation. Your goal is to empty your mind of the concerns and cares of the outer world and simply be in the presence of the sacred "I Am."

Deborah Williams is a career woman, a seminary graduate, a wife, mother, and active participant in her spiritual community. She and her husband, Dick, are also our friends. Deborah lives a full and active life. Perhaps because it's so busy, she looks forward, whenever possible, to a contemplative retreat at a local monastery. It's not simply the silence that attracts her; it's the opportunity for her to engage in the "three R's" (rest, respite, and reflection) in community with others. Her monastic experiences lift her spirit and infuse her with a new way of looking at her world. We once asked her if coming back into the "real world" was a let down. She assured us it was not, because she could bring her spiritual experiences into every aspect of her daily day. So, she said, she doesn't leave the monastery, she takes it with her. Her monastery becomes her car, home, office. Her monastery is her life with her husband, her children, her grandchildren, and her friends. Her monastery is reflective of the rhythm of life itself, and she sees it all as an opportunity to find the face of God.

Elizabeth Janeway, author of *Elizabeth Jowett*, writes, "I admire people who are suited to the contemplative life. . . . They can sit inside themselves like honey in a jar and just be. It's wonderful to have someone like that around, you always feel you can count on them."

TIME OUT:
YOUR PERSONAL MONASTERY

A monastery as Deborah Williams defined it is both a physical place and a state of being. If you created your own monastery, how would it look, what would it contain, who would it include?

YOUR INNER LIFE

An emphasis on the inner life is central to spirituality. It's usually associated with mysticism, the individual's direct experience of a fundamental reality. Author C. S. Lewis likened that experience to the contrast between reading a map of the seacoast and actually feeling the spray of the ocean on your face at the coast. Mysticism, the direct experience of the sacred, is about sensing the spray on your face.

Mysticism can bring you this experience by going beyond duality, thought, affect, or activity. It is simply being with God (which has been called "God bathing"). Soul types who are attracted to this form of spirituality seem to experience it best when they commit to contemplation as a spiritual practice. What did Jesus have in mind when he said to the scholar to love God "with all your soul?" We believe he was referring to the inner life rather than the externals of life.

Jesus' public life began at his baptism, his setting apart, by John the Baptizer. John had recently emerged from solitary life in the desert and was proclaiming himself as the "voice of one crying in the wilderness," preparing people for the coming of the Messiah. After his initiatory experience, Jesus, like John, withdrew into the wilderness beyond the Jordan River to contemplate the course of his life and his mission. After forty days alone with God and wrestling with various temptations, he emerged to begin his ministry of love and peace and justice.

The Pattern Is Consistent

Let's look at the same pattern in three other leaders whose lives changed following an encounter with the sacred. For Moses the liberator, the mystical encounter came after years of nomadic life, tending his sheep within range of the holy mountain on the Sinai

Peninsula, silently contemplating, quietly searching, and finally getting up the nerve to climb the forbidden mountain, where he encountered the sacred.

When the prophet Mohammed was forty years old, he too withdrew from family and friends and sought God in quiet contemplation in a cave near the base of Mount Hira. During his "night of power and excellence," an angel appeared and told him to proclaim the message of the one God.

In our lifetime, Nelson Mandela spent years on Robbin Island as a political prisoner of the South African government. Mandela spent most of his day in utter and complete silence, cut off from the world, languishing in his cell. For many of us, perhaps for most, this punishment would have been maddening. Those who have emerged from similar incarceration have often been physically and emotionally scarred for life. Mandela, on the other hand, left prison regenerated with a spirit of justice, truth, peace, and reconciliation, and he went on to lead a newly emergent democratic and multiracial South Africa.

In the lives of each of these spiritual leaders, whether ancient or modern, we see a pattern:

- Withdrawal from the world

- Seeking God in silent contemplation

- Experiencing the sacred through union with the divine

- Going back into the world to share the discovery with others

If you are attracted to the spirituality of contemplation, you might yourself follow a similar pattern.

Withdrawal for Renewal

The most traditional practice is physical withdrawal—"retreat," to get away—from the ordinary environment to a site or center specifically created and dedicated to exploring the inner life. These centers are often located in a bucolic setting where nature supports quiet contemplation. But whether a center is part of a sacred site made holy by pilgrims throughout the centuries or a contemporary place made intentionally welcoming to spiritual seekers, they all share a common mission: to foster the opportunity to experience transformation by stepping back from the busyness of life.

Early Christians sensed the importance of special places for contemplation and solitude, and individually they separated themselves from society. These "anchorites" went off to live a solitary life in caves in the deserts and mountains. A handful gained notoriety and a following of devotees through odd behavior, among them Simon Stylites, who chose to perch himself on top of a pillar where he prayed and fasted. Water and what little food he ate had to be hoisted up to him in baskets by means of a rope. Simon attracted quite a following of those who admired his perseverance and considered him to be a great man. By the fourth century, the monastic movement became highly organized, and it proved to be a significant way to meet the spiritual needs of those seeking insight through withdrawal from the world. Monasticism, of course, is not peculiar to Christianity; it's practiced in several of the major world religions, most recognizably at the great monasteries of Tibet.

Typically, a retreat center is hosted by a specific faith group, or other spiritual group; many centers are now open to all who seek quiet and solitude. Some prefer to make a retreat in a group—say, with your faith community—while others prefer the individual, solitary approach. If you take a retreat, you can expect refuge from the bombardment of society's stimuli. Quite often, the rules of the house don't allow television, stereo, computers, telephones, electronic games, or in some centers even superficial conversation. You will probably find a place for quiet contemplation and meditation, walking paths, a library, and rooms set aside for silence. A center might offer the opportunity to meet one on one with individuals known as spiritual directors (some people prefer the term spiritual friends) who are skilled in listening and mentoring. Retreat situations are particularly valuable for soul types attracted to the practice of contemplation.

Though many people find it helpful, it isn't necessary to physically withdraw to develop a contemplative practice. Neil Gillman writes in *Sacred Intentions* that we can "experience God's presence in many different ways and at many different moments. Sometimes God is closest to us in our moments of silent contemplation. Let those moments in." The interior life can be nourished in a church, synagogue, temple, or mosque, on a mountain top, or right in your own backyard.

Pilgrimage to the Cave

Spiritual teacher Marcia Sutton was close to fulfilling a lifetime goal of visiting the "Cave of the Apocalypse" on the Greek island of Patmos, where St. John wrote the Book of Revelation. Marcia was leading a small group on a pilgrimage to the ancient and holy sites of Greece. Along the way, they would connect with a larger tour group, which would travel by bus, visit several sites, then catch up with their luxury cruise ship for the remainder of the journey.

Marcia notes that anyone who travels internationally knows to expect the unexpected at any given time. Well it happened. The rickety bus was chugging along even slower than usual up a mountain road, and at a rest stop she queried the travel guide and learned that the bus was in such terrible shape it might not make it over the pass. Here were forty people possibly stranded, confused, unsure where they might be staying next, or even when they'd get their next meal. So Marcia gathered her small group together and they prayed like they'd never prayed before. Their prayers were answered; the driver speculated that if they could just make it over the crest of the pass, they could coast downhill to the seaport. So they all piled into the bus, miraculously it crested the hill, and as they coasted down they passed many Greek ruins, including the Temple at Delphi, where the oracle once delivered sacred messages. Rejoicing, they coasted into the port just fifteen minutes before the ship was scheduled to leave. More bad news: their luxury liner had been commandeered to assist in an emergency situation. Another ship of questionable quality was waiting for them, but the trip to Patmos would have to be canceled. Needless to say, the tour group was despondent. Not one to be easily defeated, Marcia gathered her group together and let them vent their frustrations, then they all prayed for guidance, and as they prayed, she willingly surrendered going to Patmos.

Shortly after the prayer session, she learned from the travel guide that by taking a ferry from Rhodes they could reach Patmos late in the evening. She asked her group if they still wanted to go, but only one stepped forward. Undaunted, she and her companion set off for Patmos. After a night's rest on the island, they managed to visit the great Monastery of St. John, see the priceless icons the monks had collected over the centuries, and make their way to the Cave of the Apocalypse. The small cave had been hollowed out of a rocky hillside, and because it was off season, there were very few tourists, so she and her companion had the cave nearly to themselves. Not just for the fleeting moments the original itinerary allowed, but for hours of glorious contemplation.

Sitting within its confines, as she prayed, chanted, lit candles, and even wept over her great joy at achieving a life's ambition, she came to a greater realization of why she was there. It was because of God's love. She knew it was that love that had brought her there; it was that love that always carried her along, even through uncertain times; it was that love that opened new doors for her even when other doors were closed. It was that love, as St. Paul said, that never fails; that love from which nothing can ever separate us. So, what could have been the vacation from hell for Marcia turned into a pilgrimage of joy. Here in this sacred cave, she had a sublime experience of love, through surrender and trust in God's will for her.

■ ■ ■

Today, there is a growing renaissance across faith boundaries of interest in the sort of contemplative practice you would find in a retreat setting. Recently, we were made aware of this cross-cultural interfaith emphasis in two distinct settings. The first example is in the opening words of the mission statement of a prominent church: "We believe in one God, known to us in Jesus Christ, also known by different names in different traditions." The second was in a retreat offering sponsored by the Society of St. John the Evangelist, at their monastery near Harvard University. Titled "What the Spirit Is Saying to the Churches," the retreat focused on how contemporary Christianity has been enriched by its exposure to other faith traditions. The brochure commented that "in the increasingly pluralistic culture of the 21st century, this cross-fertilization is very likely to continue." The mission statement and the retreat brochure are both reflective of a growing trend that reaches across faith lines to seekers, no matter their tradition.

CENTERING PRAYER

One of the most popular forms of nourishing the interior life is called centering prayer, where union with the pure consciousness of God comes through a structured format. Specific and regular times are used to be still and empty your mind of thoughts, concerns, judgments, and fears, quietly centering yourself in the presence of the sacred. Thomas Keating and Basil Pennington are outstanding contemporary teachers of the centering prayer movement, which shares similarities with Transcendental Meditation and other Hindu practices. Two twenty-minute time segments are set aside each day in which you use a special word, or mantra, to still the mind. Keating describes the process in *Open Heart, Open Mind*:

Consciousness is like a great river. On the surface, our superficial thoughts and experiences glide by like boats, debris, water skiers, and a myriad of other things. The river itself is the participation God has given us in his own being, but we are ordinarily unaware of it because we are absorbed with what is passing by on the surface. In centering prayer, we begin to shift our attention from what is on the surface to the river itself.

The use of silence and a mantra helps to return the mind to a wordless state. The philosopher J. Krishnamurti, like Keating and Pennington, agreed that during meditation one should "observe" thoughts as they come up, but not engage with them, instead simply noticing them as they float on by and bringing the self back to the river of consciousness.

TIME OUT!

Meditation isn't mysterious or "other-worldly." Try this simple ten-minute process:

1. Make yourself comfortable. Sit erect with your spine straight, your feet on the floor, your hands relaxed in your lap. (The reason for all this? Nothing spooky. If you're comfortable, you're less likely to think about your body.)

2. As you breathe in, count to four. As you breathe out, count to four.

3. Once you've regularized your breathing, become quiet and say to yourself, *I'm listening, God.*

4. Continue the breath pattern, resting in God. When you are ready to end your meditation, quietly say, *Thank you, God.*

Reflect for a few moments about your experience. Was it easy for you? Was it difficult? Did you "hear" anything? Did you feel anything?

SACRED READING

Lectio Divina is an ancient form of contemplation that is regaining popularity. Let's first look at three common "nots" of the Lectio:

1. The practice is not a form of Bible or sacred text study.

2. It is not similar to reading sacred writings for purposes of edification.

3. It is not a practice in which one prays the scripture in common.

Although Lectio fits more than one soul type, it's primarily a practice of soul-centered spirituality. It cultivates listening deeply, to hear "with the ear of our heart," as St. Benedict described it. Lectio, as we know it, developed during the scholastic period when things tended to become compartmentalized, so though this process is divided into four distinct parts, it is intended to lead effortlessly from one part to the other.

How does it work, and what can you expect from this practice?

The process has four stages, with Latin titles: *lectio, meditatio, oratio,* and *contemplatio.* The first stage is *lectio,* where you begin with a reading from scripture (or from a spiritual book). A phrase or a word that pops up or emerges from the text (that is, one that captures your attention) is identified and focused on. In the second or reflective step, *meditatio,* you ponder the words of the text, which leads spontaneously into *oratio,* or affective prayer. The process culminates in *contemplatio,* resting in the presence of God where the rhythm of practice and being are in harmony. This four-step meditative process has been used for centuries, and more and more contemporary spiritual communities are gathering to practice it. Of course, it's an individual activity as well. The process itself suggests an ascending motion, a gentle oscillation back and forth, spiraling upward as we first encounter, and then rest in, the presence of the divine.

SACRED SOUND

At first glance, sound would seem to be antithetical to contemplative practice. Yet the ecumenical community of Taizé, in France near the Swiss border, offers worship experiences that focus not only on silence but also on light and hauntingly beautiful chant. The Taizé community was begun in 1940 by Brother Roger Schutze, who wanted to found a community that would reach out to help people escaping the horrors of Nazi persecution.

Following World War II, the community, which had grown to seven brothers, continued to provide respite and refuge for all who sought God. Over the years, their distinctive form of contemplative worship, study of scripture, silence, and small groups attracted tens of thousands of pilgrims, among them thousands of youths, who are spiritually nourished by their experiences. They take the spiritual practices they learn at Taizé, especially the hauntingly beautiful chants, with them when they return home. Taizé meditative chant experiences are now common across North America.

We entered the large sanctuary of the city church for the Wednesday evening service: light came solely from two hundred flickering candles, and we were soon immersed in the hypnotic sound of Taizé mantralike chants, repetition of words and phrases, sung over and over. This form of worship engages the mind, bathes the senses, penetrates to the soul, and finally brings you into the changeless presence of God. It was a profound spiritual experience.

SACRED MOVEMENT

Physical postures also feature prominently in contemplation practices: walking, kneeling, sitting cross-legged, lifting up the hands, crossing the arms over the chest, making the sign of the cross, vocal prayer, silent prayer said with the lips but not with the voice, fingering prayer beads, and chanting sacred words. Hindus and Buddhists use complex physical postures during meditation. In Tibet, they use a form of walking contemplation as they perambulate around a *kora*, a wooden frame filled with decorated prayer drums. Each drum has a prayer written over and over on a long strip of paper and then tightly wound around the drum. Each spin of the drum releases a prayer. Catholic monks often read their daily office as they walk around the monastery grounds. Pilgrims of many spiritual traditions are willing to walk long distances, sometimes in an organized procession, to reach a holy shrine, such as Lourdes in France, Walsingham in England, Compostella in Spain, the Golden Temple in India, or Mecca in Arabia. You can meditate just as easily by sitting comfortably in a chair.

SACRED GEOMETRY

A walking meditation that has attracted widespread attention is found in the "sacred geometry" of the labyrinth, an archetypal form that allows a direct experience of God. The form emerged from the concept that life is a journey, a journey into wholeness, always moving closer and closer toward God. The idea is that we are all exactly where we should be on the spiritual path. A labyrinth is a model for that path. It is usually in the form of a spiraling circle, meant to demonstrate that life, with all its twists and turns, inevitably leads us to our spiritual center, and to a heightened sense of life. Walking the labyrinth takes us out of our ego-self, into the center of our being, and then back to the world of affairs.

(The labyrinth is frequently confused with a maze, but the two couldn't be more different. The purpose of the labyrinth is to show that there is a single path leading to the divine, a path that leads in and also leads out. The purpose of a well-constructed maze, on the other hand, is to confuse, confound, and give you a sense of being lost.)

The design in France's Chartres Cathedral is the most recognizable labyrinth. It was primarily used four times a year in the Middle Ages at festivals to honor the Virgin Mary. Pilgrims removed their shoes at the entrance to the cathedral and walked barefoot up the length of the nave until they reached the geometric design embedded in the floor. As they stepped into the labyrinth, they danced round and round, following the various permutations of the design until they reached the center. There they would kneel, arms outstretched in prayer, asking the Virgin to refresh their souls. The Chartres design became popular; Rheims has a variant of it, though there it was used as a way to symbolize rebirth at Easter. Another, similar to Chartres, is carved on a pillar in Lucca Cathedral in Italy.

The labyrinth is not a European Christian discovery. The Italian painter Botticelli observed that labyrinths were used by the ancient Egyptians. In North America, Hopi Indians employed at least two forms, one nearly round and the other square, both said to represent Mother Earth.

The contemporary resurgence of the labyrinth is largely the work of clergyperson Lauren Artress of Grace Episcopal Cathedral, high atop San Francisco's Nob Hill. Her fascination with the labyrinth at Chartres, and its use as a potential spiritual tool, led her to introduce it to a new audience in North America. Artress revived the practice as a way of creating a bridge between traditional and nontraditional forms of meditation, and to serve as a symbol of healing and wholeness. The labyrinth has become so popular that the San Francisco cathedral now has two. The first, inside the building, takes the form of a huge octagonal carpet, with the geometrical design woven in purple on a white background. It's used every day the building is open. Another identical labyrinth is outside the cathedral, embedded in the paving of the plaza. This outdoor labyrinth (which was funded by a family of another faith tradition) is available twenty-four hours a day and serves the needs of people when the cathedral is closed.

SACRED DANCE

Dance is yet another way to use the body to achieve union with the divine. David is said to have danced before the Ark of the Covenant. The celibate Shakers in America were known for their music and their distinctive dancing, or "shuffling," as they called it; founded by "Mother" Anne Lee in the eighteenth century, they lived in highly organized communities. Their dances, which were part of the worship, were in keeping with their sense of orderliness and followed definite patterns and steps. The shuffles were named the "Square Order Shuffle," the "Quick Step Manner," and "Simple Gifts." Some were solemn and stately, while others were livelier with undulating rhythmic patterns. Men and women lined up on opposite sides of a room facing each other. They then danced three paces forward, three paces back, with a double-step in between, all intended to achieve mystical union.

The Simple Gifts shuffle was introduced by "Father" Joseph Brackett in 1788. The accompanying song, which has become popular once again, includes allusions to the dance steps:

> 'Tis the gift to be simple, 'Tis the gift to be free.
> 'Tis the gift to come down where we ought to be.
> And when we find ourselves in the place just right,
> 'Twill be in the valley of love and delight.
> When true simplicity is gained,
> To bow and to bend we shan't be ashamed.
> To turn, turn will be our delight,
> Till by turning, turning we come 'round right.

Sacred dance is part of Middle Eastern practices as well. The Mevlevi Order of Sufis traces its origins back to thirteenth-century mystic Mevlana Jalaluddin Rumi of Anatolia, Turkey.

Rumi developed the theme of an essential unity that goes beyond the duality of life. Contemplation, he said, was the best way to discover and experience the harmony and peace of the universe.

For seven hundred years, his followers have used dance as a con-templative form of attuning themselves to God. Frequently referred to as "whirling dervishes," the devotees, men and women, wear ankle-length white garments with fitted tops and very full skirts. Using precisely orchestrated hand and foot motions, they twirl first in a measured pace and then faster and faster into a state of ecstasy, during which they expect to experience the divine.

EASTERN AND WESTERN SPIRITUALITY COME TOGETHER

Can you hear the themes that are developing in the symphony of contemplation? So many instruments from so many traditions, yet they work together to produce a harmonious song. Soul-centered spirituality in the Western world is reflected in the teachings and practices of Protestant mystics such as George Fox, Jacob Boehme, and John Wesley; as well as such Catholic mystics as Teresa of Avila, John of the Cross, and Meister Eckhart, all of whom are be-ing rediscovered and are enjoying unprecedented popularity. East-ern spiritual practices also are finding ready acceptance in the West. The insights of Tibetan masters, Hindu gurus, Sufi mystics, and the ancient Jewish contemplative tradition in the Kaballah find a recep-tive audience among those who are able to combine practices of East and West in their spiritual lives and yet maintain the integrity of their own faith traditions.

Interest in Buddhism has commanded the most attention. Think of the popularity of *Living Buddha, Living Christ*, by the Viet-namese Buddhist monk Thich Nhat Hanh, in which the author draws parallels between the teachings of Buddha and Christ and portrays them walking the same path. He finds the Christian sense of mindfulness through the Holy Spirit a healing source, while in Buddhism he sees unqualified love as revealed in its compassion for all living things. Thich finds a strong sense of communal spirit in both, and an equal emphasis on living one's life through spiritual practice. Or consider the Eckhart Society, whose aim is to promote Meister Johann Eckhart's spiritual writings as they affect Christian thought and practice, and to further his teaching as a contribution to interfaith dialogue. It's insightful to learn that the Eckhart Society's founders got their initial support from their Buddhist spiritual director. Catholic author Richard Chilstrom, in his small book on the spirituality of Eckhart, *God Awaits You*, says that Eckhart "has become a significant bridge between the Eastern and Western mystical traditions. . . . At times, it is hard to differentiate his thought from that of a Zen Buddhist."

Alan Lew, a respected rabbi, found that the contemplative practices of Zen Buddhism led him to rediscover his Jewish roots. From Zen he learned that spiritual practice permeated every aspect of his life, in the simple acts of bathing, sleeping, and working, as well as meditating or listening to "spiritual" lectures. Lew brought to Judaism that same concept of the importance and pervasiveness of practice. He comments: "Judaism is, in fact, a spiritual practice of great depth and integrity. Daily prayer, *shabbat* [keeping the Sabbath], *kashrut* [following dietary practices], the yearly spiritual cycle—these are the lineaments of an ancient and disciplined practice." Lew teaches meditators how to achieve union with a higher reality through focusing on Hebrew letters. He represents a growing segment in Judaism known as "Jubus" (pronounced jew-booz), those who are Jews by birth but are attracted to Buddhist practices. Jubus see no conflict in this connection with Buddhism, and many prominent teachers of Buddhist practice in America are Jewish.

The contemplative or mystical practices we've explored are not intended to replace faith communities or to become a new religion. They are instead, as Jesus intimated, one more element in learning the love of God, self, and neighbor. As Bernard McGinn, one of the foremost scholars of contemplative practices, has commented, "The idea that mysticism floats free is something that Christianity, Judaism, Islam and other religions would react against because their mystical teachings are part of the complex of being a Christian, Jew, or Muslim. . . ."

Regardless of their faith tradition, soul-centered types are attracted to these and other contemplative practices, which are intended to strengthen a holistic understanding of the oneness of life.

SOUL-CENTERED ASSESSMENT

Are you are a soul-centered type? Take this short assessment to see.
Read each statement, and rank it using this scale:

> 3 = very important for me
>
> 2 = important for me
>
> 1 = not so important for me

1. Silence is important to me on my spiritual path. _____

2. I agree with Jesus' statement that the kingdom of God is within. _____

3. It's important to take time each day for quiet reflection. _____

4. I would enjoy spending time at a retreat center. _____

5. I would like to go on a pilgrimage to a sacred place. _____

6. God is present in me at all times. _____

7. I like reading about mystics and others who experience God directly. _____

8. I see life as a journey into God. _____

9. I believe my purpose in life is to achieve union with the divine. _____

10. It's more important to listen to God than to speak to God.

    _____

11. I'm interested in learning contemplative meditation techniques. _____

12. It's important to empty my mind of random thoughts so that I can rest in God. _____

Add up all your responses. Write the total number here: _____

SOUL-CENTERED CONTEMPLATION PRACTICES

1. Start a regular daily practice of a few minutes of silence, or quiet contemplation, each day.

2. Learn a simple meditative technique, such as observing and counting your breath as you inhale and exhale.

3. Find a special place where you can be quiet. Remember that a retreat need not be in a church, monastery, or center; it can be in any place where you experience the presence.

4. Listen to sounds (might be from a CD) that bring you into the presence. They might be a chant, a musical composition, the sound of wind chimes, or the lapping of waves along the seashore.

5. Use your body to calm your mind and bring you a sense of the unhurried rhythms of life. Examples: walking a labyrinth, Tai Chi, yoga, sitting quietly, petting an animal companion, dancing, running, walking, riding, gardening, smelling flowers.

6. Establish a regular "sabbath," or quiet day, preferably each week, in which you put aside your busyness and replace it with quiet relaxation.

7. Read books, magazines, or Web pages about one of the great mystics. What were their transforming experiences? What do those experiences say to you?

8. Keep a journal in which you record what you hear when you silently listen to the sacred. You might want to record your dreams in the journal as well, if you feel God says something to you during sleep.

9. Look at a sacred image, an icon, a painting, a mandala, or a sunrise or sunset—anything that reminds you of the oneness, beauty, and wonder of life.

10. Listen or talk to others about the power of soul-centered practice. This could mean enrolling in a meditation class, listening to a lecture or sermon, practicing centering prayer with a group, or chatting online about contemplation and contemplative practices.

8

Mind-Centered Spirituality

The Practice of Awareness

"Wake up," Jesus said to them,
"You've slept long enough."
LUKE 22:46

PROFILE OF THE MIND-CENTERED SOUL TYPE

You often see life as a puzzle to be solved, and you prefer orderly thought and intellectual exploration. Discovery based on knowledge is significant in your spiritual search, so words, mental constructs, and complex ideas provide spiritual nourishment. You expect intellectual substance from a spiritual community. Listening is important. Interested in the meaning and intent of sacred writings and literature, you are likely to be attracted to an in-depth study of theological topics. For you, greater knowledge can lead to greater understanding, and greater understanding to increased awareness.

Kyle," his father calls as he knocks on his son's bedroom door, "wake up!"

Kyle answers through the closed door, "I don't want to get up, Dad."

His father shouts back, "Get up, it's time for school."

"I don't want to go to school," Kyle replies.

"Why not?" his father asks.

"Let me give you three reasons," Kyle responds. "One, school is a bore; two, the kids don't like me; and three, I hate school."

His father shouts back, "Then let me give you three reasons why you must go to school. One, it's your duty to go; two, you're thirty-eight years old; and three, you're the principal. So wake up!"

Mind-centered spirituality is about awareness, *aka* attention, concentration, recollection, or mindfulness. In this chapter, we use the term *awareness*, but you can substitute whatever term you prefer to mean being consciously present. No matter what you call it, awareness is about waking up spiritually, looking around, and taking in what you see nonjudgmentally, without evaluation. On his final night on earth, Jesus asked several of his followers to keep watch for him so he could withdraw into the silence of the garden at Gethsemane for a time of intense prayer. But when he came out of the garden, he found them sound asleep. "Wake up," he shouted, "you've slept long enough." He had expected them to be fully conscious in their thinking, listening, speaking.

This mind-centered spirituality invites you to see the wonders of God all about you, without preconceptions or considerations. The great Spanish cellist Pablo Casals said, "Each second we live is a new and unique moment that never was before, and never will be again." The possibility of utter transformation through practicing awareness is offered each moment to each of us in a unique way.

TIME OUT!

When you arise in the morning, make a determination—
perhaps in a short prayer or affirmation—to let go of your
worries and concerns and simply be in a state of awareness.
During the day, jot down any worries you experience. At
the end of the day, review your list.

Does it indicate that you truly believe God is in charge,
or did you actually believe that you were in charge?

The next morning, surrender everything on your list,
saying: "God, I give you these worries and concerns. I'm
ready for you to remove them. Thank you, God."

ADS TO ENTICE THE MIND

A magazine ad featured a man with two pieces of tape over his
mouth. The caption read: "Jesus came to take away your sins, not
your mind." In our superficial culture the use of the mind in spiritual practice is too often neglected. Mind-centered spirituality, we
hear, is too heady, too brainy, too evaluative.

If this third type of spirituality were merely about collecting
mental data and being judgmental, we'd agree. However, as Sir John
Eccles (a renowned scientist who won a Nobel Prize for brain
research) tells us, the brain is not a producer of energies as once
thought, but the receiver that picks up impulses and transposes
them into data that our ego-consciousness can then comprehend.
The energies themselves, he says, come from a realm inaccessible
to measurement, from a purely spiritual level that can only be experienced. Sir John is saying that perhaps the brain plays a vital role
in awakening to the presence of God.

"The God Ad" campaign, developed by the Smith Agency of Florida, produces "heady" ads as a positive way to awaken people spiritually. The donor's purpose was simply to get people thinking about God, so the agency placed contemporary, slightly irreverent, thought-provoking ads on ten thousand billboards across the country. Funded by an anonymous individual—and we mean so anonymous even Oprah Winfrey can't get this person on her show—the campaign uses brief, punchy, attention-getting one-liners, each signed by "God." Here are some of the ads already in use:

"Need directions? God."

"We Need to Talk. God."

"Do You Have Any Idea Where You're Going? God."

"I Loved the Wedding. Invite Me to the Marriage. God."

"What Part of 'Thou Shalt Not . . .' Didn't you Understand? God."

Does this attention-getting stuff work? Apparently so, judging by the e-mails and letters the Smith Agency receives. Even CNN did a piece on the project. One woman, asked by a reporter about her initial reaction to seeing these ads, aptly replied, "Thank God."

AWARENESS

Awareness is the beginning of transformation. It's letting go of one's preconceived concepts of reality, which is not always easy. In fact, it's quite difficult for most of us because we are so invested in the drama, events, and circumstances of our life, past, present, and future.

In his book *How to Want What You Have*, Timothy Miller says, "Attention [awareness] is the intention to live without reservation in the here-and-now." Some have called this "being there." Being there means staying in the here and now rather than being distracted by your problems. Being there for others means latching on to what is important in what a person is saying, and resisting the temptation to steer the conversation in the direction you think it ought to go. It means staying with them and not leaving them for your own agenda.

All living traditions honor awareness as a key component in spiritual growth. It's what Paul meant when he urged people to "fix your attention on God. You'll be changed from the inside out. . . . God brings the best out of you [and] develops well-formed maturity in you" (Romans 12:2). Bringing out the best is what this Jewish mother wanted to do: When her son comes home from school each day, she quizzes him not about what he learned, but what questions he asked. It's why Islam stresses prayer five times a day to keep people spiritually awake. It's the perception of God that Puritan leader Jonathan Edwards called "Divine Mind." In all of these ways, awareness is important.

Alan Watts, in *The Wisdom of Insecurity*, says that awareness is beyond definition and description: "Most people imagine themselves to be fully enough aware of the present already, but . . . this is far from true. Because awareness is a view of reality free from ideas and judgments, it is clearly impossible to define and write down *what* it reveals. Anything which can be described is an idea, and I cannot make a positive statement about something—the real world—which is not an idea. . . . What is true and positive is too real to be described, and to try to describe it is like putting red paint on a red rose."

Although, as Watts notes, awareness may elude definition and description, the process does not. Whether you're just beginning or you've been at it for years, conscious awareness can help you in finding the answers you seek.

FOCUSING THE MIND

Two ways of increasing awareness that have gained enormous popularity in recent years are the inspirational magazine *Daily*

Word and the use of *koans* or stories from Zen Buddhism. *Daily Word*, published by Unity, is a good example of attentive focus. We're mentioning this little magazine because it's the most widely read devotional magazine in the United States. More than one million people reflect every day on the short, pithy messages intended to strengthen their awareness of the presence of God. We've met people from many religious traditions who "swear" by *Daily Word*. The daily topics are intended to reframe or refocus the mind.

In a similar way, Zen Buddhism raises awareness through spiritually based *koans*, stories that are designed to shake us out of our normal thought patterns. Through koans, the practitioner of Zen ideally realizes that everything comes from mind and that truth is basically intuitive. Here's an example:

> A monk asked the teacher Kegon, "How does an enlightened one return to the ordinary world?"
>
> Kegon replied, "A broken mirror never reflects again, fallen flowers never go back to the old branches."

Odd? Nonsense? In Zen, words, concepts, and meanings have no clear, linear logic. It is only in your reflection on them that the spiritual meaning reveals itself.

The Ayurvedic doctor Deepak Chopra writes in *Ageless Body, Timeless Mind*: "The quality of one's life depends on the quality of attention. Whatever you pay attention to will grow more important in your life." Most people display symptoms of lack of awareness (attention) at one time or another. After all, it's challenging to stay fully in the moment. It's like putting your car on cruise control and losing sight of where you're headed. Being awake and alert isn't all that easy; in fact, it's a tough spiritual challenge, maybe one of the greatest we face.

PARADIGM, TRANSFORMATION, AND METANOIA

For you to become more aware requires a "paradigm shift," a way to think and act differently. A paradigm is a set of rules and regulations that establish boundaries, and it's within those boundaries that problem solving takes place. Your current paradigm—the one you accept and operate under—acts as a filter that screens and categorizes information as it comes into your mind. It determines not only how you see things but *what* you see, and it governs how you think and interpret. For example, if your paradigm is "No matter what I do, I can't seem to get ahead," then this is the framework within which you interpret what happens to you.

Once you accept an interpretation, it becomes reality for you. You become so accustomed to your own mind-set that you don't usually question it; it's your reality. So when you're quizzed or challenged about a particular habit of yours, you are likely to answer, noncommittally: "That's just me." You can't see what you're doing because to do so requires stepping outside of your own paradigm, and that's not easy. But when your paradigm does shift—perhaps as the result of a shock, or an epiphany—it's as if a veil has been lifted from your consciousness. You see the same things, but you see them from a new perspective.

At some point in your life, you probably felt that life would be better if only "they" would change—your partner, your children, your friends, your boss—and you set about trying to change them. But here's the rub: even if they all changed, *you'd still be the same*. Any real change must be in you, not in them. If you consider how difficult it is to change you, what real chance do you have of changing anyone else?

Change, which is central to transformation, takes place in you and through you. Once you have indeed changed, you'll probably find that they are still the same, but you'll see them in a new light.

The word *transformation* comes from the Latin *transformare*, which simply means to change shape or form. This is what often happens when *metanoia* (Greek for a changed or a new mind) takes place. You see the world in a new and fresh way, and how you live life is transformed.

Early followers of Jesus felt they were called to experience metanoia to fully grasp the idea that the kingdom of God was "at hand," right now, right here, beyond the rigidities and prejudices of the human mind—to experience a profound new way of seeing life. In *The Gnostic Gospels*, Elaine Pagels quotes Jesus as saying that "the lamp of the body is the mind," and when you "recognize what is before your eyes . . . what is hidden will be revealed to you."

Metanoia was an ancient way of saying "Change your thinking, change your life."

Forget Rule One

Rubber-faced funny man Jim Carrey spent many years resenting his parents. The subtitle of Mark Lasswell's *USA Weekend* article about him read: "For 40-something superstar Jim Carrey, Rule 1 is: Never let them see the real you. Rule 2: Grow up! It's time to forget Rule 1."

Jim started his career as a teenage stand-up comic in Toronto, Canada. His father was out of work. His mother, who was often ill, came to depend on Jim as the family breadwinner. This is tough for any kid. Jim knew it was his duty, but it made him smolder inside. Both of his parents are now dead, yet when he gave interviews he'd spend a lot of the time being angry at them for robbing him of his childhood. That lack of childhood affected his adult behavior.

Now he's learning to lay that aside, as he portrayed in his film *Liar, Liar*. It's a film with a message: "Parents, don't B.S. your kids." Laswell commented that Carrey has "grown up personally." Carrey said: "I have done enough thinking for five lifetimes, I want to work and lay some things down that mean something to me." Rule two is to grow up and forget rule one. That's a paradigm shift. It's metanoia in action.

It often takes someone or something to challenge your thoughts and ideas to cause a paradigm shift. The shift can't happen until you're willing to listen. Until then, no one can assist you. What does help is self-observation, having your eyes wide open about where you're coming from and what your motives are. It's about observing and understanding what you observe, but without judgment. Why? Because judgment obscures true understanding. It may take something drastic to wake you up, but when you do wake up, watch out. Jacques Lusseyran, in *Against the Pollution of the I*, said, "Permit me to say without reservation that if all people were attentive [aware], if they would undertake to be attentive in every moment of their lives, they would discover the world anew. They would suddenly see that the world is entirely different from what they had believed it to be."

Here's a bit of wisdom from the cartoon character Calvin of "Calvin and Hobbes." Calvin says to Hobbes, "Know what's weird? Day by day, nothing seems to change, but pretty soon . . . everything changes."

Clay Walker Turned a Negative into a Positive

Country music singer Clay Walker has become acutely aware of the power of change. He became a new dad, he produced five number one top hits, and both of his country music albums went platinum; it was a great series of rapid changes, all by the young age of twenty-six. One day his right leg seemed to give out, and his right arm was tingly. He soon got to the point where he couldn't even hold a guitar pick with his right hand. Then he developed a face spasm that lasted for eight weeks.

Clay was diagnosed with multiple sclerosis, a disease that affects the central nervous system. It can hit people at different levels, and when Walker got his diagnosis it appeared that he might never regain the use of his right arm or his right leg. "I didn't know," he said, "if I'd get to see my daughter grow up." Before the onset of MS he spent the majority of his time with his music. His life slowly began to change. He's got a new perspective now; he's become more concerned about others; he's redeveloped his interest in sports; and he wants to make better and lasting relationships with family, friends, and fans. At age thirty-three, he's ready to release his ninth album. In 2002, he formed his own Band Against MS Foundation to raise money for research. Merchandise sold at his concerts funds the foundation.

He still has MS, but he's avoided another major attack, and he's gotten back 95 percent of the use of his right leg. Dealing with MS has helped him shift his paradigm; he sees reality differently now. Clay Walker is a living example of the power of positive change through awareness.

Awareness Can Mean Accepting God's Will

Awareness changed Jean Taylor's life. In November 1993, as she and her husband were planning their retirement trip, she began feeling tired and weak. Medical tests revealed ovarian and colon tumors.

She writes, "I will never forget the day when I got the diagnosis. I sat on my bed for a while, frightened and praying for healing. But the longer I prayed, the worse I felt. I had no answer." Then she remembered what Catherine Marshall, widow of the great U.S. Senate chaplain, Peter Marshall, had said, that the most powerful prayer was the one Jesus prayed on the night before he died, "Not my will be done, but yours, God." She realized that she might die, so she prayed, "Okay, God, I can't deal with this alone, so whatever happens I leave it to you. If I live or if I die, I'll accept it." The heavy weight of fear that was oppressing her vanished, and she was aware of a sense of peace.

After surgery, the doctor offered little hope for recovery; the cancer continued to grow and spread. Five days later, she was back in the hospital, because the chemotherapy treatments had produced a severe reaction. Her kidneys shut down, she contracted pneumonia, and she had a mouth full of thrush, a painful virus in the mouth and throat. She was fitted out with a feeding tube to her stomach through the chest wall and sent home. Several months later she went into remission. Doctors were amazed, as only 10 to 15 percent of ovarian cancer patients survive. Her brother asked her where she got the courage to deal with all she went through. She told him, "It wasn't courage because I wasn't afraid. It was faith knowing that God was in charge." Eight years later, she's still cancer-free, but owing to another set of maladies she's not pain-free: "I cope by asking God's help in accepting them and in finding ways to work around what I can't change. When I realize that I'm not coping, I pray like Paul for 'that peace which passes all understanding.'"

Jean's healing came when she gave up judgments and became aware of the presence of God. In that moment, she found peace and serenity. There was nothing she had to "do," no special skills or techniques or strategies. Her simple release of thoughts, fears, hopes, and judgments allowed her to be in God, yet still be actively engaged with the world around her. This is the gift we are offered in the spirituality of the mind; all that is required is a little willingness on our part.

Brother Mandus, an English mystic, once described this as the "most important realization of all . . . [that] there is one mind of God, and that the human mind, conscious and subjective, is the gift of Divine Mind for use in a personal way."

Awareness Creates Spiritual Giants

John Wesley, a don at Oxford University, had his life transformed at a meeting in Aldersgate Street, London, just a few minutes' walk from St. Paul's Cathedral. It was about 8:45 in the evening and he was listening to someone reading Luther's preface to the Letter to the Romans, when suddenly he felt transformed; as he put it, his heart was "strangely warmed." His faith now made sense to him, and he experienced an overwhelming awareness that God had changed his life. He promptly moved from the rigid confines of the established church to teach and preach to the poor, the disaffected, and the alienated. Thousands responded to his message, first in Britain and then in North America. Though it wasn't his intention, so powerful was the simple message and the commitment of Wesley and others that it became the worldwide Methodist movement. All this from simply listening, from being aware, and being open.

Taylor and Wesley discovered what Nicholas Herman (better known as Brother Lawrence), a lay monk of the Carmelite order, found four hundred years ago. He wrote about it in his small, power-packed spiritual classic, *The Practice of the Presence of God*. In it he describes how he found transformation in the common round of daily tasks, cleaning, polishing, and sweeping floors, as well as through the moving words and beautiful chanting of the monastic services. "I do nothing," he wrote, "but abide in his holy presence, and I do this by simple attentiveness and a habitual, loving turning of my eyes on him. This I call a wordless and secret conversation between the soul and God."

THE ROLE OF LISTENING IN GREATER AWARENESS

We've seen in the stories in this chapter that awareness includes some form of active listening. Let's now consider active listening as a source of spiritual growth. There's an adage that God gave us two ears and one tongue so that we can hear more and talk less. This goes hand in hand with another one, that it's hard to hear when you're preoccupied with your own thoughts.

What interferes with active listening? Some say the culprit is the "monkey mind." This is an ancient concept that refers to the mental chatter, the "yada, yada, yada" that prevents us from being and doing our best. It's a term used to describe how human consciousness has the capacity to jump all over the place, like jabbering monkeys in the trees.

Monkey mind—those random, trivial thoughts that lead our mind down a dead-end trail—tries to prevent us from making the radical changes required for spiritual transformation. We're all afflicted with it at times, but the more we're aware of it the more quickly we learn to recognize its characteristics and avoid being trapped by it.

Jesus constantly had to remind his followers to pay attention, to listen. Though they appeared to be attentive, he knew that their minds were filled with thoughts that blocked the full impact of his message. On at least a dozen occasions recorded in scripture, he confronted them about it. He'd look them directly in the eye and confront them, "Are you listening to me? Really listening?" (Matthew 11:15); and "Pay attention to what you hear" (Mark 5:24). A native American proverb says, "Listen or thy tongue will keep thee deaf."

You cannot really listen while you are doing something else at the same time. Anna, a college student, thought she could. On her way across campus to get a soft drink, she saw her friend Ed sitting on a bench near the soft drink dispenser, busily reading something. Anna got some coins out of her pocket and dropped them in the machine, at the same time saying to Ed matter-of-factly, "How are you doing?" She later found out that Ed had responded, "I just got a letter from my mother. She has a malignancy, and I think I'm going to have to go home to help her." Anna said, "I didn't hear him; I got my drink and I said to Ed, 'So, what do you have planned for the weekend?' I hadn't heard a thing."

An anecdote is told about Francis of Assisi, who accompanied the soldiers on the Fifth Crusade to Jerusalem to recapture the holy sites. Through several misadventures—or divine appointment—Francis was taken prisoner and found himself face-to-face with the Sultan of Egypt. The sultan knew of Francis and had him brought to his tent for a discussion about God. Francis didn't talk much, maybe out of fear, but he did listen for hours as the sultan talked about his intense love for God. Francis was profoundly moved by this encounter; when he returned to Italy he taught that no one had a monopoly on God's love. His former views of what the spiritual life should be were transformed simply by actively listening and neither judging the sultan nor debating with him. Francis, in turn, has affected countless others, helping them open up to awareness through listening, hearing, and absorbing. Attentive awareness is not only for medieval monks and enlightened sultans; we need it today.

When we listen to somebody completely and attentively, we listen not only to the words but also to the feeling of what is being said—all of it, not just a portion of it. One of the most valuable things we can do for one another is to listen to each other's stories. Someone once said the reason we engage so politely in conversation is that we're not listening to the other person so much as waiting for them to stop, so we can have our say. It's like the Fleetwood Mac song "Don't Stop" (thinking about tomorrow). We're so busy thinking ahead we fail to realize what's really happening now. Listening is not simple; it takes time for the chatter in the head to quiet down. There's truth in the saying that wisdom is the result of spending a lifetime listening, when what you'd rather be doing is talking.

PRACTICING AWARENESS

Living expectantly in the "now," simply being there, is at the heart of awareness. Practicing awareness can be a liberating experience because we choose a different, more open state of mind in which growth is possible.

In his book *Awareness*, Anthony De Mello offers some excellent advice on practicing awareness, and he recommends putting it into practice "a thousand times." He says to identify those negative feelings in ourselves but understand that these are feelings within us and are not part of our external reality. By changing our inner reality, he says, we change everything.

MIND-CENTERED ASSESSMENT

Are you are a mind-centered soul type? Take this short assessment to see. Read each statement, and rank it using this scale:

> 3 = very important for me
>
> 2 = important for me
>
> 1 = not so important for me

1. Spiritual growth comes from being consciously aware. _____

2. I prefer spiritual practices that stretch my mind. _____

3. The concept of God as Divine Mind is appealing to me. _____

4. The more awake I am, the more aware of the sacred I become. _____

5. I can understand more about God through study. _____

6. I prefer well-ordered, intellectually stimulating worship experiences. _____

7. Effectively handling monkey mind is necessary. _____

8. I enjoy attending classes and lectures on spiritual subjects. _____

9. Listening without judgment is important in spiritual growth. _____

10. I enjoy learning spiritual insights from the established faith traditions. _____

11. I prefer spiritual practices that have been developed over the years. _____

12. I prefer written prayers, meditations, and affirmations. _____

Add up all your responses. Write the total number here: _____

MIND-CENTERED SPIRITUAL PRACTICES

1. Establish a habit of daily prayer around a particular prayer (Lord's Prayer, Prayer of Jabez, Prayer of St. Francis, Serenity Prayer), or use set prayers (for example, the monastic daily "offices," which are forms of morning and evening prayer such as found in *The Book of Common Prayer* or *A Gnostic Book of Hours: Keys to Inner Wisdom*). Give yourself at least thirty days to get into this important positive habit. Several forms of daily offices can be downloaded from the Internet.

2. Create a habit of daily inspirational readings from sacred scripture or the writings of spiritual leaders. Many books, tapes, and magazines are available.

3. Create (and illustrate) a book of your own prayers and meditations.

4. Find a "prayer partner" with whom you can discuss your spiritual journey. This could be one to one, or by telephone, e-mail, chat room, fax, and so on.

5. Enroll in a class on comparative religion, contemporary theology, or a similar spiritual topic. Alternatives are listening to a lecture, sermon, or a message that stretches your mind and your imagination.

6. View a film or look at (or meditate on) a fine piece of art that might inspire you to think about sacred themes or the meaning of life.

7. Visit Websites that focus on religious and spiritual topics. There are also many discussion groups and chat rooms that offer an opportunity to explore spirituality in greater detail.

8. Practice listening to others, trying not to judge or evaluate what they are saying. This is a tough one, but it's good practice for beginners because it reveals to us how many of our 86,400 seconds each day are given over to judgment rather than awareness.

9. Use techniques that help focus the mind: listening to pat-
terned music (Bach, Mozart, the Beatles, chant), fingering
prayer beads, listening to or reading spiritual writings.
10. Deal with "monkey mind." When the mind is filled with
random thoughts that prevent awareness, don't examine or
entertain them; bless the thoughts, and let them pass by.

9

Strength-Centered Spirituality
The Practice of Commitment

However many holy words you read, however many you speak,
what good will they do you if you do not act upon them?
BUDDHA

PROFILE OF THE STRENGTH-CENTERED SOUL TYPE

You see life as an opportunity to create a better society,
to build the kingdom of God on earth. For you, spiritual
growth means being able to serve others, and it begins
with a personal commitment to oneself. Serving others
might take the form of support, advocacy, or direct
action in relation to a moral or ethical issue, or it might
be manifested through helping others in compassionate
support. Motivated by a strong sense of idealism, you
want to participate actively in meaningful issues. This
may be a one-on-one activity or participating with a
group. Formal belief systems are less important than the
vision of a transformed world. Often the initiator of
change, you believe spiritual growth can best be gauged
by what you do rather than what you say or believe.

Betty's mother overheard her young daughter talking to herself in the backyard. Betty wanted to try out for the school softball team, and she was practicing hitting the ball—or, let's say, she was practicing *trying* to hit the ball. She said, "I'm the greatest softball hitter in the world." Then she threw the ball in the air and swung at it. Missed. That didn't bother her, and she repeated, "I'm the greatest softball hitter in the world," and she threw the ball and swung at it. Missed again. She tried it several more times, and never hit the ball. She paused, walked around the yard in deep contemplation, and then stopped. She looked carefully at the bat. Then she studied the ball. Time to try again. She said, "I am the greatest softball hitter in the world." Up goes the ball, swing, and no hit. Then her eyes lit up, and she said, "I got it! I'm the greatest softball *pitcher* in the world."

Loving God with all your strength, one of the four spiritualities Jesus mentioned, is not a one-time event but a series of committed efforts to try and try again. The first thing to understand is that this practice involves giving yourself to something greater than you. Kazuo Inamori, renowned business leader and creator of advanced ceramics technology for electronic components, observed that commitment is an action of the heart that is motivated by a sincere desire to serve the world.

COMMITMENT

Webster defines commitment as "the act of giving oneself to a higher charge or trust." Spiritual commitment, in the sense in which we're using it, is "disciplined practice," not the quick fix of life's problems that most people desire. It is a spirituality defined by stability, consistency, and dedication, to which you bring all your strength. It is a holistic process rather than fragmented; it is intentional rather than haphazard.

Fundamentally, commitment is a spiritual practice stemming from a conviction that the love of God can be brought to the world by service to others. A key element in the practice of commitment is the desire to share your gifts and graces with others through acts of service and charity, or doing justice: "Whenever you do commit to one of these things to someone who is overlooked or ignored, you do it as for me" (Matthew 25:40, paraphrased). So convinced was Jesus of the power of commitment that he constantly pressed his followers to get beyond their narrow parochial outlooks and to let nothing stand in their way.

The process of commitment has three distinct steps:

1. A decision to surrender one's personal desires to a higher power in order to serve others

2. A way to strengthen your commitment, often in community with others

3. Becoming alive with a passion to share the benefits of commitment with others

TIME OUT!

A commitment to serve others can be in the form of a simple act of kindness. This commitment could be just a few minutes. It's not the amount of time that's significant, but your willingness to give to others of such a precious resource as time.

- Make a commitment today to phone, e-mail, or write to someone you haven't talked with for a while.

- Take a few moments to talk with a neighbor, or your postal carrier, or a service provider.

- Share some time with an animal companion, caress your cat, or run with your dog.

> After committing your time, set aside a few minutes to reflect about what you did and how you felt about it. Do you think spiritual growth can come from simple commitments such as the one you made?

HERE'S WHY WE KNOW ABOUT THEM TODAY

Let's look at a few examples, some ancient, some more recent, of individuals who practiced spiritual commitment.

Abraham Said Yes to God

Can you imagine Abraham's bewilderment when God instructed him to find a new home for the people of Israel in Canaan? Abraham agreed to do it, but he had no idea where Canaan was, nor how to get there, nor what he'd find when he got there. Once he figured out the general direction, the journey proved to be one disaster after another. The people who had formerly supported him began having seconds thoughts, especially when not enough food was available. They questioned why they were on this journey, was Abraham right, did he really hear from God. Yet he (no doubt with a lot of heavy grumbling of his own) persevered in his commitment and finally did lead them to Canaan.

The Prince Who Waited

The Indian Prince Siddhartha withdrew from his life of wealth and privilege to seek the sacred through contemplation. The stories say that after searching in vain for an answer, he finally sat himself down under a bo tree and promised not to budge until he got an answer. He said, "Though skin, nerves, and bone shall waste away, and life-blood itself be dried up, here I sit till I attain enlightenment." And there he sat, susceptible to desires, cravings, hunger, thirst, ridicule, and sufferings of every kind. Still he sat there, till his commitment bore fruit and he came to the realization of the divine he was seeking. This was the point of realization at which Prince Siddhartha became Sakyamuni, the Buddha. With his new understanding of enlightenment, he traveled throughout India teaching freedom from human suffering through awakening to selflessness and the interconnectedness of all life.

He Made the Right Move

When Mohammed concluded that staying in Mecca was hindering the spread of his message, he was guided to relocate to Yathrib, three hundred miles north. His followers were put out by this decision, because they were convinced that Mecca was the city most receptive to his teachings. Undeterred, Mohammed made the strategic shift to Yathrib. This journey is celebrated as the "Hejira," a seminal event in the emergence of Islam. It made Yathrib so famous that it was renamed Medina, City of the Prophet. Here his teachings reached a high level of acceptance, the first mosque was built, weekly communal prayers were instituted, and it was at Medina that the regimen of daily prayers and emphasis on giving alms and support for the poor began.

Here I Stand

In the sixteenth century, reformer Martin Luther was ordered to the German city of Worms and commanded to recant his heretical views. He refused to give in. His commitment to his beliefs and ideas was so strong that, at the risk of death, he told his accusers,

"Here I stand; I can do no other." This had a profound effect not only for people in the sixteenth century but for millions of Protestants in the nearly five centuries since.

The Pope and the Painter

About the same time in Rome, Pope Julius wanted the ceiling in the Sistine Chapel repainted. The chapel had been built by Sixtus IV in 1473 and the ceiling was painted blue spangled with stars. In 1508, Julius convinced Michelangelo to paint it, and the artist chose for the themes the creation, Adam and Eve, and Moses and the Ten Commandments. Every day, Michelangelo was hoisted up by ropes to the scaffolding, where he had to lie on his back to paint. Can you imagine the commitment it took? Day after day mixing the paints, twisting his neck into uncomfortable positions, holding his arms up to paint until they became numb. Julius, a military man with a strict sense of discipline, expected things to be done his way and without too much delay. Michelangelo, a meticulous artist, would not be rushed by anyone, and he took four years to complete the job. In the movie *The Agony and the Ecstasy*, there were frequent scenes where the impatient Pope would shout up at the scaffolding, "When will you make an end to it?" Michelangelo would peer over and emphatically shout back, "When I am finished." Each had a commitment to excellence: Julius to getting the job done expeditiously, Michelangelo to getting it done to his satisfaction. Their joint efforts manifested in the magnificent ceiling of the chapel.

Twenty-two years later, Michelangelo was commissioned by another pope to paint the Last Judgment on the wall behind the altar. This magnificent chapel is visited by thousands of art lovers and tourists every year. We were among the tourists during the time the frescoes were being restored, and a humorous incident took place. Artists high up in the scaffolding, using modern techniques in their total commitment to reclaim the artwork from the ravages of time, conversed freely back and forth, and their conversations could be heard. The hundreds of tourists who packed the room were committed to viewing the whole magnificent spectacle, and verbalized with "oohs" and "aahs." Conversation ranged from erudite comments of connoisseurs to the more commonplace "You sure don't find anything like this in Kansas."

But there was a steward on duty with a different sense of commitment. This is a holy place, and in his mind silence should prevail in holy places, so he made it his job to shush groupings of people. But no one paid serious attention to him. Frustrated at not achieving silence, he took a drastic measure and dragged a large, heavy table loudly across the floor to the center of the room. He noisily climbed up on the table and waved his arms in every direction shouting at the top of his lungs: "Silenzio! Silenzio! Silenzio!"

Bill W., Bob S., Sam S., and AA

Commitment is not reserved to the past or to restoring the past. The twentieth century produced one of the most successful examples of commitment: Alcoholics Anonymous. AA has been influenced by the practices and beliefs of Bill Wilson of New York, Bob Smith of Akron, Ohio, and Sam Shoemaker of Philadelphia. Doctor Bob's early meetings relied heavily on prayer, Bible study, devotional literature, and quiet meditative times. Bill W., on the other hand, did not come from a religious background, but his desire to overcome his alcoholism brought him into contact with Sam S., pastor of Calvary Episcopal Church, who had been deeply influenced by the spiritual work of Carl Jung.

Sam's Jungian studies and his experiences with the Oxford Group led him to conclude that the aspect that was the most needed in AA was spirituality, committing to something greater than oneself, or surrendering to a "higher power." Princeton professor Robert Wuthnow relates the story of "Frank," who found his spirituality in AA. "I openly admit," Frank said, "that if I'm going someplace to talk to people about God, I'll go to an AA meeting. If

I want to talk about spirituality, I'll go to AA." Frank, with millions of others, discovered that spirituality and commitment go hand in hand. The value of commitment is also encouraged in the work of such successful support groups as Weight Watchers, Narc-Anon, Alateen, and Gamblers Anonymous.

If you are associated with, or have been associated with, a self-help group, did you find a measure of spirituality in your group?

Agnes Who?

You may not be familiar with her under her given name of Agnes Bojaxhiu, but you probably have heard of her by her religious name, Mother Teresa of Calcutta, the Nobel Peace Prize recipient. She was loved and admired by scores of people, from the famous to the humble, because of her commitment to help the poorest of the poor, especially those who literally lived on the streets of Calcutta and had no support system. She and her Missionary Sisters of the Poor ministered to the seriously ill and dying, providing them with food, shelter, and medicine, but most important with a sense of personal dignity. The heart of her message was, "Go and do something beautiful for God."

Can you recall a time that you did something beautiful for God?

SO WHO'S HELPING WHOM?

This concept, often referred to as "servant leadership," is as old as religion, but it has been given new meaning as the result of a single man, Robert K. Greenleaf. "The difference," Greenleaf writes in *The Servant as Leader*, "manifests itself in the care taken by the servant—first to make sure that other people's highest-priority needs are being served. The best test, and one difficult to administer, is: do those served grow as persons; do they, while being served, become healthier, wiser, and freer, are they more likely themselves to become servants of others?"

Greenleaf sees Jesus as a significant model for serving others. In John 13:1–6, Jesus, as he often did, teaches by example. During the Passover feast he suddenly got up, removed his outer garment, and wrapped a towel around his waist. Then he poured water into a large bowl and startled his followers by going to each one of them, washing their feet, and drying them with the towel. "I have set the example," he said to them, "and you should do for each other exactly what I have done for you." Through this simple act, Jesus gave us a quantum leap in understanding how we can grow spiritually.

Providing Simple Joy

You are surrounded by those who have grown spiritually by serving others. The form of service you choose doesn't have to be in the Mother Teresa style. Thousands of people each day—maybe you are among them—quietly "do something beautiful for God." Joseph Charles, "the waving man of Berkeley," didn't intend to become famous. But when he died at ninety-one, hundreds of people attended his funeral, including Berkeley's mayor, Shirley Dean. She remarked, "Everyone came to him because he stood in front of his house waving, with a big smile, that came from the heart." His purpose was to spread joy, and he did it simply, every day for thirty years: by standing at the busy intersection of Oregon and Grove Streets, waving and smiling at every car and pedestrian who passed by. It's estimated that he waved to one hundred million people, an average of forty-five hundred per day. He did it not for praise but as his way of serving others. What is more basic than a smile and a wave of the hand? Yet by this commitment, Joseph Charles touched the lives of millions, and most of them returned the smile and waved to him.

The Homeless, Kids, and Peanut Butter

Then there are the young teenagers, Jeremy and Cindy, who were appalled at the number of street people who were going hungry in their midwestern city. They said, *But they need so much help, what can we do?* One day, on their own, they made up a batch of peanut butter sandwiches, wrapped them in plastic, went to an area where the homeless congregated, and handed out sandwiches to the needy. Soon other teens joined them, and in a short time they were offering hundreds of sandwiches each day. City officials heard about what was happening and tried to put a stop to it, citing health issues as the reason. The kids felt they were doing meaningful work, and they contacted the newspaper. Motivated by a heart-wrenching piece of journalism, the city decided to assist the kids and made available basic health guidelines, supervision, and encouragement. Did the kids do this for the publicity? No. They did it because they wanted to do something for someone else. This is an example of how a small endeavor can yield great results. What small things could you do?

Compassion in Action

Another remarkable practitioner of commitment was Mychal Judge, a chaplain to the New York City Fire Department, who first achieved fame because of the spiritual care he provided to families of TWA Flight 800 victims. Father Judge had a reputation as a hands-on minister of compassion in his service-related activities. A recovering alcoholic himself, he lived out the values of the twelve-step program as he helped others find their sobriety.

Judge had a loving personality and an easy smile, and he became a healing presence for many, as a supporter of justice for the gay and lesbian community and a tireless worker on behalf of police officers, firefighters, and families in crisis. He once commented: "In seminary, you can get all the theology and scripture in the world, and you land in your first parish, and you find out it's you—the personality and the gifts that God gave you that count." He was among the first emergency responders to the World Trade Center disaster, and one of the first of those responders to lose his life.

Mychal Judge's life was celebrated at a funeral service at St. Francis of Assisi Church in midtown Manhattan. A mosaic of mourners reflected the diversity of his ministry, as the poor; the affluent; politicians; ordinary citizens; and celebrities such as Bill, Hillary, and Chelsea Clinton all sat side by side at the service, reflecting on the work of this ordinary priest made extraordinary through his service to others.

Walking for Peace

Mildred Norman, better know as "Peace Pilgrim," found her form of commitment through walking for peace. It came about as an inner urging. "I felt a complete willingness, without any reservations, to give my life, to dedicate my life to service," she said. "I tell you, it is a point of no return. After that you can never go back to completely self-centered living."

She first began walking in the summer of 1952 on the 2,050-mile Appalachian Trail. Over the years, she traveled more than twenty-five thousand miles across the United States, usually alone. During her walks, she shared her simple, basic message: that the way to peace is to overcome evil with good, falsehood with truth, and hatred with love.

She dressed distinctively in navy blue slacks and shirt, tennis shoes, and a navy blue tunic with pockets all around the bottom, in which she carried a comb, a folding toothbrush, a pen, and the small blue leaflets she passed out on the way. Her tunic had the words PEACE PILGRIM on the front, and WALKING COAST TO COAST FOR PEACE on the back. She never had to purchase another tunic, since all her clothes, for the rest of her life, were gifts from admirers. She carried no money and was resolute that she would not beg for food or for anything. If no food was offered to her, she went without or found it in the wild. She slept where she could—in bus stations, out in the open, or in homes when she was invited. She talked to anyone who would listen about the practical things one individual could do to work for world peace and for inner peace.

Peace Pilgrim totally relied on the goodness of God to sustain her and her message. Her mission was covered in the media around the world in magazine articles, in radio stories, and on television. She said, during an interview, if "one little person, giving all of her time to peace, makes news, many people, giving some of their time, can make history."

What a Neighborhood!

History was made quietly and gently by Fred Rogers, the star of public television's "Mister Rogers' Neighborhood." Millions around the globe mourned his death in February 2003 at the age of seventy-five. Rogers, in his unassuming manner, made the lives of children happier through his forty years of commitment. Through more than eight hundred television programs he carried out his work to "make goodness attractive."

Fred Rogers was not devoid of other options. He was born into wealth and educated at the best schools; he was a classically trained pianist and an ordained parish minister who chose to specialize in children's ministry. "All of my interests," he said, "have been used in the service of children and their families. To find an avenue to use all the gifts you have been given is a blessing. I have been particularly blessed."

Mister Rogers taught generations of children, and their parents, how the world—a good world—can and should be. He said, "Essentially, we are very deep and very simple, and our society so often encourages us to be shallow and complicated, but the more we can attempt to look for the deep and the simple in our life and in our neighbors' lives, the greater satisfaction our lives will have." Fred Rogers was a national treasure and a testament to the idea that service can bring great joy and satisfaction.

COMMITTING TO YOURSELF

The practice of commitment ultimately comes down to personal commitment to yourself. It's a call to your own authenticity that requires you to see yourself as capable of change and willing to grow in spiritual strength to bring about positive change, if called to do so, in the lives of others.

David Owen Ritz, spiritual leader of the Center for Positive Living in Sarasota, Florida, said, "When we give of ourselves in service, [God] will always use us to promote the growth of others in unexpected and wonderful ways; but we will always be the main beneficiary of that transaction."

The Psychiatric Times (October 2000) reported that there is a very real correlation between good mental health and commitment. The study noted that making a spiritual or religious commitment may actually aid in recovery from substance abuse and depression, as well as reduce health risks. Apart from these potential blessings, there are added benefits such as personal fulfillment, satisfaction, exhilaration, and sense of worth that would be impossible to find in the pursuit of merely personal goals.

Commitment can be as complex, as involved, or as lengthy as you want it to be. If you are a beginner in this practice, we recommend that you start slowly, with simple short-term commitments to serve in a cause or activity to which you are particularly attracted. Remember what Mister Rogers said about simplicity. Try a number of service opportunities. See which ones fit you best before making a longer commitment of your time.

STRENGTH-CENTERED ASSESSMENT

Are you a strength-centered soul type? Take this short assessment to see. Read each statement, and rank it using this scale:

> 3 = very important for me
>
> 2 = important for me
>
> 1 = not so important for me

1. I agree that my spiritual growth begins with a personal commitment. _____

2. I think it's more important to walk the walk than to talk the talk. _____

3. Spiritual and religious groups must be involved in helping the needy, poor, and disadvantaged. _____

4. Personal commitment is an important factor in deepening spiritual growth. _____

5. I think spirituality can be expressed through demonstrations about public issues. _____

6. I would be attracted to a spiritual leader well known for his or her views on social justice. _____

7. I enjoy sermons, talks, and lectures that support a specific point of view about a public issue. _____

8. I'd attend a vigil that calls attention to a public stance about a societal issue. _____

9. When a spiritual group supports people who are oppressed, they are doing God's work. _____

10. I believe writing letters or cards to public officials expressing my views is part of my spirituality. _____

11. I believe that commitment means giving of myself completely to something larger than me. _____

12. One committed individual can help to make this world a
    "better place." _____

Add up all your responses. Write the total here: _____

STRENGTH-CENTERED COMMITMENT PRACTICES

---

1. Find a "hero" who can teach you about commitment through the way he or she lives or lived. What do you see in the person's life that demonstrates, or defines, commitment? Your hero could also be a cause you believe in. Read about it, and learn as much as you can.

2. Make a list of positive habits you've developed or want to develop consistently. Alternatively, adopt a new positive habit that requires commitment.

3. Start using short affirmations or prayers that reinforce a commitment you've made. Two examples: "I am determined to see God in this situation." "I can do all things through Christ, who strengthens me."

4. Keep a daily journal of the commitments you've made, and record the results and feelings about keeping (or not keeping) your commitment.

5. Volunteer for a short-term commitment in a service organization or in a spiritual community, even if it's for one or two hours.

6. Say your prayers or meditations at the same time each day.

7. Fast for one meal, and give the money you'd have spent on food to a cause you believe in.

8. Write a letter, postcard, or e-mail in support of a cause that has spiritual significance for you.

9. Participate in a gathering in support of a cause you favor— a vigil, march, or demonstration.

10. Find a movie (such as *Norma Rae* or *The Agony and the Ecstasy*), or see or read a play (such as Bertolt Brecht's *Mother Courage*), or look at artwork (such as Picasso's *Guernica*) that represents commitment to you. What can it teach you?

PART III

I Know Where I'm Going

Your Life Map

Follow, follow, follow, follow,
follow the yellow brick road.
FROM *THE WIZARD OF OZ*

A small section of Lombard Street in San Francisco has become a famous tourist attraction due to the way it's laid out. Instead of running straight, this street is designed as a series of hairpin turns that wind like ribbon candy down the steep hill. You must be fully conscious and aware to make the sudden corrections that allow you to drive safely and joyfully down this unusual street!

It is just such an adaptive quality that makes life *mapping* more powerful than life *planning*. Plans don't provide effective ways to deal with the zigs and zags of life's challenges. Maps—simply by charting the territory from here to there—do just that.

10

Constructing Your Life Map

The feeling remains that God is on the journey, too.
TERESA OF AVILA

As you create your Life Map in this chapter, you are charting a direction for your life on the basis of your own unique spiritual DNA and your soul type. You may not be where you want to be right now, and you may have to zigzag every now and then, but you're on your way. Having this information before you empowers you to make any necessary course corrections so that you live life in an authentic manner.

Have your journal or Life Map notes on hand; you need to refer to what you've already written down. You'll be doing some copying, so have clean pages in your journal or a note pad available. If you haven't completed the work in Chapters Two through Nine, this is the time to go back and finish it!

Through the work in this chapter, you put all the pieces together, remembering that as you do this work you are charting the course for your spiritual journey.

EXERCISE YOUR CREATIVITY!

This Life Map is intended to be a personal charter for your future. Once they've completed their map to their satisfaction, many people like to make it extra special by adding a bit of artistry, such as handwriting it in calligraphy, or using a special typeface, or decorating the initial letters of each section, or designing a special border, or illustrating each section or key word to make it more vivid. Post your map where you can see it regularly. Make copies, and keep one with you or near you for ready reference.

You created it, so make it special, and make it uniquely yours!

TIME OUT (OPTIONAL): BEFORE YOU START . . . DISCERN

Reserve some quiet, reflective time to be still and to listen, and try to discern the will of God for you. Arthur Caliandro says that God does have a will for us in our lives, and even during the most confusing and worst times, we can "tune in" to God's will for us.

An auto's license plate revealed God's will to a spiritual writer. It happened to Frederick Buechner (beek-ner) twenty years ago. He was in his car worrying about his anorexic daughter, and as a car drove by, Buechner read the license plate: "T R U S T." He said, "Of all the . . . words that I needed to most hear, it was that word *trust* . . . telling me, 'trust your children, trust yourself, trust God, trust life; just trust.'" He trusted, and his daughter recovered.

He mentioned this in a talk he gave. A man, who had heard the talk, came to his home and handed him that very plate. He was a bank trust officer, hence T R U S T. It hangs on Buechner's wall as a reminder to trust. He writes: "Trust that if God is anywhere, God is here, which means there is no telling where God may turn up next—around what sudden bend of the path if you happen to have your eyes and ears open, your wits about you, in what odd small moments, almost too foolish to mention."

- God does "speak" to you, and continually sends you hints and clues that are much more powerful than words.

- God might communicate to you through a subtle leading or prompting, a thought, an idea, an inner urging, or a moment of realization.

How will you know that you have discerned God's will? Here are three basic guidelines:

1. God's voice always clarifies.

2. God's voice never condemns.

3. God's voice brings a sense of peace.

Now let's begin creating your Life Map.

MY SPIRITUAL IDENTITY

You are so much more than you appear to be. We know scientifically that you are a living organism with your own unique DNA that determines who you are as a physical entity. And you are more than that, for there is a part of you that is often overlooked, your spiritual identity. As you begin creating your Life Map, your spiritual identity will become clearer to you.

Who I Am

In Chapter Two, you were introduced to the idea that spiritually you are a valuable person with enormous potential, growing and changing even as you read this sentence.

Reflect on the real you. How would God describe you?

Do this: in your journal, write a positive statement beginning "[God] would say that I am _____ ."

My Positive Qualities

A prolific inventor, Thomas Edison said, "I have not failed. I have just found ten thousand ways that won't work." People often define themselves according to their perceived failures, weaknesses, or inadequacies, but from a spiritual perspective, that's not the truth.

Do this: list five positive qualities about you that describe you as a spiritual being.

1.

2.

3.

4.

5.

What's in a Name?

There are myriad names for God. If you haven't chosen one, turn back to Chapter Two and pick one or more that you feel you can use comfortably. In your Life Map, from now on use that name or those names when you refer to God. On a sheet of paper, use the name(s) to complete the next sentences, even if you've chosen "God" as the answer.

Do this: my name for God is _____ . I chose this name (or these names) because _____ .

WHAT'S IMPORTANT FOR ME?
MY CORE VALUES

In Chapter Three you identified, defined, and prioritized your core values. Now it's time to incorporate that crucial material as the very nucleus of your spiritual DNA.

Do this: list your top three to five core values, with their definitions. _____

_____

_____

_____

_____

_____

My Interests and Passions

Quick check: what often happens in life is that your values are most vividly displayed through your interest and passions. If you had unlimited energy, vibrant health, and financial freedom, how would you use your time? Or, to say it another way, what interests you so much that you completely lose all sense of time while you're engaged in it?

Do this: list several (three to five) of your most compelling interests and passions. _____

_____

_____

_____

_____

_____

Now compare these interests and passions with your chosen defined values. Is there a fit? Do these activities truly reflect your foundational values? If they do, then be thankful that your "doing" is reflected in your "being." If you're not sure they really fit, consider whether these interests and passions can be replaced by others more appropriate. You want to give your doing an opportunity to fully cooperate with your being.

WHY AM I HERE?
MY UNIQUE LIFE'S PURPOSE

As we discussed in Chapter Four, you must have an identified purpose. Look about you in your world. If you see people who are successful, happy, peaceful, creative, and satisfied, they are people who have discovered why they are here, their reason for being, their purpose or mission in life. You too can create an authentic life filled with that wonderful soul-lifting sense of wholeness. Give yourself to your purpose. Don't shy away from it or let go of it. Let your life be purpose-driven.

Do this: write out your purpose statement.

_____

_____

_____

_____

_____

Quick check: review your written statement, in light of these questions:

- Does it represent the best that is within me?

- Does it truly reflect my core values?

- Does it reflect my interests and passions?

- Am I inspired to action by my purpose statement?

Give it a test. When you've honed your statement, share it with someone else—spouse, partner, friend, or associate. Is your purpose clear to others? Does it need a bit more honing? If so, do that before you move on.

WHERE DO I WANT TO GO?
MY VISION FOR THE FUTURE

What your life would look like if you carried out your purpose is your vision, your glimpse into the future.

TIME OUT

Look at a picture on a table or anywhere nearby. Think of the frame as your purpose; it stays firm and steady. Pictures in a frame can be changed over time, even though the frame remains the same. A vision is in essence a set of pictures, and as new pictures come into being they can replace the old pictures or add to existing ones. These pictures are simply reflections of your values.

Do this: write out your vision statement. _____

_____

_____

_____

_____

_____

_____

Quick check: ask yourself, Do the words "feel" right? Do they capture the essence of my picture? How would I feel if it became reality?

Make any changes you feel are appropriate. Remember, visions can and should change as you get the results you're dreaming of.

You have uncovered the key components that are at the core of your spiritual DNA: your values, your purpose, and your vision. Your next step is to find appropriate ways of expressing this spiritual DNA through your soul type and practices.

THE CIRCLE OF LIFE

Do this: transfer your soul type assessment scores from Chapters Six through Nine, and enter them in the appropriately named quadrant in the Circle of Life.

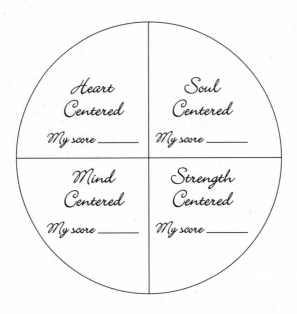

The circle represents your wholeness as a complete being. There's no cause for concern if your scores are not equal in each quadrant; they don't need to be. You can be a balanced individual and still have a clear preference as to your soul type. The quadrant in which you scored highest is your primary soul type. If you scored high in two or more quadrants, then both are your soul types.

My primary soul type is _____

My secondary soul type is _____

SOUL-TYPE PRACTICES

The practices associated with each soul type are ways you can grow as a spiritual being. Through these practices, you'll feel more satisfied, more at peace, and more joyful, and in so doing you create a more authentic experience of life.

Do this: list the specific spiritual practices related to your primary soul type—either from Chapters Six through Nine, or some of your own—that you're currently using. Some of the examples were

Say Grace not only before meals but also before all activities for which you are thankful.

Start a regular daily practice of a few minutes of silence, or quiet contemplation, each day.

Practice listening to others, trying not to judge or evaluate what they are saying.

Volunteer for a short-term commitment in a service organization or in a spiritual community, even if it's only for one or two hours.

You need not do all the practices associated with your soul type in order to feel whole. The object is not to keep score; it's to create an authentic life that is based on your spiritual DNA. You may find one or two practices so compelling that they meet all your needs for spiritual expression.

Recommendation: avoid overcommitting. Start with one or two practices from your primary soul type and develop them, track your results in using them, and then move on to another. If you overcommit, you'll end up focusing on the practice rather than on what the practice is intended to accomplish.

CHECK OUT OTHER PRACTICES

The practices we listed for your primary soul type (at the end of the corresponding chapter of Six through Nine) are practices that particularly support that type. But if you feel drawn to and wish to explore other practices from the other soul types, or from other sources, please do so.

List them.

_____

_____

_____

_____

_____

Goals and Objectives

Goals and objectives are useful, but our experience has been that sometimes people get more concerned with them than with the spiritual practice. Nonetheless, it is appropriate to set goals and objectives if you view them as benchmarks or a way to measure how you're doing with a practice. Goals are the broad general outcomes you'd like to produce, while objectives are measurable aspects. Both can be changed at any time.

Here's an example. Sarah Ferguson, the Duchess of York, says it isn't necessary to "give up that bit of cake" to get your weight under control. She reminds us through Weight Watchers—the organization she represents—that the real challenge is making realistic goals.

Your *vision* is to be a healthier person. Your *goal* is to lose weight in order to be healthier. Your *objective* is the number of pounds you want to lose, by a "doable" date. This goal and objective are realistic and attainable. Once the objective has been reached, you can create another.

In terms of spiritual goals and objectives, they might look like this:

Goal: I want to incorporate silence more effectively in express-ing my spirituality.
Objective: I will sit silently for ten minutes each morning for the next two months.

At the end of two months (or whatever time frame you've chosen), if you want to keep the same goal you can change the objective to, say, fifteen minutes twice a day.

Do this: on the basis of your vision and soul type, list the goals and objectives you wish to establish for your spiritual practices.

_____

_____

_____

_____

IMPLEMENTING YOUR MAP

Now that you have completed writing out your Life Map, you can use it to guide you in your life's decisions. Most of us will need to be reminded of our commitments: anchoring, repetition, and positive self-talk can be helpful tools to assist you.

Anchoring

"Anchoring" is a technique intended to strengthen your commit-ment to your values, purpose, vision, and spiritual practices. Anchoring can be done through an object, an image, a word or phrase, a sound—anything to remind you that you are going in the right direction.

Rep-Rep-Repetition

In physical exercise, repetition is a key to successful anchoring. Spiritual work is no different, so in some spiritual practices one is often asked to repeat something a certain number of times. Repetition reminds, deepens, and reinforces. For the next few months, we recommend what follows:

Repetition and Your Core Values

Concentrate on one core value for a week, or concentrate on a different core value each day for a week. Verbally repeat a value and your definition, several times. Use your journal to keep track of how you are doing.

Did you actually live into that value? If so, in what ways?

If not, what simple step can you take to get back on track?

Repetition and Your Purpose Statement

Your purpose statement is like your personal constitution. Keep a copy of it with you to remind yourself regularly what you're about. As a spiritual practice, repeat your purpose statement in the morning, or several times during the day as a reminder.

Repetition and Your Vision Statement

Each evening, repeat your vision statement before you go to bed. If you have a regular evening prayer time, include your vision as part of this activity.

Repetition and Spiritual Practices

At the end of each day, review the spiritual practice or practices you've chosen for that day. Enter in your journal how you did.

Repetition and Partnering

Recall that we framed our examination of soul types in terms of Jesus' recommendations about ways to love God: with heart, soul, mind, strength. But he also said to love your neighbors as yourself. Jesus was offering a highly practical technique for spiritual practice. That is, find a partner, or group, with whom you can share your spiritual journey.

Positive Self-Talk

The technique of "positive self-talk" motivates you to remember all the good, worthwhile results you're trying to produce through your practices. Stop and reflect on why you're doing what you're doing, how far you've come, and how you will continue to have success. Become your own coach or mentor through positive self-talk or affirmations.

PERIODIC CHECKUPS

It's easy to fall into a routine, even with spiritual practice. Periodically, take time to check in with yourself to make sure your practice is really alive. Do this quarterly or at least every six months. Mark your calendar as a reminder. If you have the opportunity to use a retreat situation for a checkup, all the better. If not, create your own retreat situation in your home, a park, or some other place where you can quietly review your Life Map.

Here are some pointers to use during your retreat.

Are You Living Your Core Values?

Check your values against your relationship, or lifestyle, or current job. How well are they aligned? There's a direct relationship between the level of satisfaction in these areas and your personal values.

When you're faced with a major personal decision or tough choice, pull out your core values for help in deciding what to do.

Periodically look at some of the choices and decisions you've made. Were they consistent with your core values? If you had to make a decision over again, would it be the same? What would you change to bring the decision into harmony with your values?

Are You Living Your Purpose?

Every so often, take time to review and evaluate your personal purpose statement to keep you in touch with the direction you've charted. Although fundamentally it is timeless, it needs to be periodically reviewed as you grow and change. Here are some questions to ask yourself:

- Is my purpose statement based on timeless principles? What are they?

- Does it represent the best that is within me?

- Do I feel good about what this purpose statement represents?

- Do I feel a sense of direction, challenge, and motivation when I read it?

Are You Living Your Vision?

Use your vision statement to empower yourself and to help you set achievable goals, both long-term and short-term. Refer to your vision statement in your daily planning. This ensures that you regularly spend time on things that truly matter to you. Remember, your personal vision represents your commitment to create the results in your life that you deeply desire.

What skills and strategies will help you live up to the goals and objectives you've set within your vision?

Does your vision statement still inspire you?

Are you adding new "pictures" to the frame of your vision?

EPILOGUE

Follow Your Bliss!

Historian and teacher of comparative religion Joseph Campbell once said that the life you ought to be living "has been there all the while waiting for you." Campbell writes: "If you follow your bliss, you put yourself on a kind of track that has been there all the while, waiting for you, and the life that you ought to be living is the one you are living." He was observing that the search for meaning is really a search for the experience of life.

The journey you have been on, discovering your spiritual DNA, is a first step in the process of experiencing life wholly, totally, authentically, joyfully.

RESOURCES

Robert Norton and Richard Southern
2269 Chestnut St., #621
San Francisco, CA 94123
(888) 801–1186
Email:cds@growingcongregations.org
www.growingcongregations.org

■ ■ ■

BeliefNet

Features articles on God, faith, prayer, the nature of spirituality,
society and ethics, surveys, and so forth.
www.beliefnet.com

Centering Prayer

Contemplative Outreach spiritual network committed to living the
contemplative dimension.
www.centeringprayer.com/frntpage.htm

Daily Word

Stories, messages, and thoughts to support one's individual faith.

Celebrity articles included.
www.unityworldhq.org/daily_word.htm

God Ad Campaign

Article on spiritual billboards donated by local billboard companies
as a public service.
www.newsherald.com/archive/religion/mm030399.htm

Human Genome Project

What the project is; its progress, history, and goals; issues associated
with genome research.
www.ornl.gov/TechResources/Human_Genome/home.html

Labyrinth

See Veriditas

Lectio Divina

Introduction to the practice of personal and group Lectio Divina.
www.valyermo.com/ld-art.himl

Mysticism in World Religions

Explores the mystical literature of the great religions.
www.digiserv.com/mystic/

Peace Pilgrim

Information on her twenty-eight-year pilgrimage for inner and outer
peace; includes writings.
www.peacepilgrim.net

Shakers

Through technology in their religious tasks, they created many in-
novations and inventions.
www.hancockshakervillage.org/old/shakers.html

Spirituality and Health

Spiritual practices, self-tests, news, essays, reviews, products on many aspects of spirituality.
www.spiritualityhealth.com

Taizé Community

The ecumenical, international community in Taizé, France.
www.taize.org

United Religions Initiative

Promoting enduring, daily interfaith cooperation to end religiously motivated violence.
www.uri.org

Veriditas: Voice of the Labyrinth Movement

Grace Episcopal Cathedral in San Francisco is the home of the worldwide labyrinth movement.
www.gracecathedral.org/labyrinth/index.shtml

World of Religion According to Huston Smith

Article on Smith, who has devoted his life to the study of world religions and likes them all.
www.motherjones.com/mother_jones/ND97/snell.html

BIBLIOGRAPHY

Armstrong, K. A History of God. New York: Ballantine, 1993.

Barker, J. F. The Power of Vision. New York: HarperBusiness, 1991.

Barker, J. F. Paradigms: The Business of Discovering the Future. New York: HarperBusiness, 1992.

Bass, D. (ed.). Practicing Our Faith: A Way of Life for a Searching People. San Francisco: Jossey-Bass, 1997.

Beattie, M. The Lessons of Love: Rediscovering Our Passion for Life When It All Seems Too Hard to Take. San Francisco: HarperSanFrancisco, 1995.

Brussat, F., and Brussat, M. A. Spiritual Literacy: Reading the Sacred in Everyday Life. New York: Simon & Schuster, 1998.

Caliandro, A. "How to Discern God's Will." Sermon on Marble Collegiate Church's Website: http://63.147.212.191/sep2000.html.

Cameron, J. The Vein of Gold: A Journey to Your Creative Heart. New York: Tarcher/Putnam, 1997.

Campbell, J. The Power of Myth. New York: Anchor, 1991.

Carroll, L. Alice's Adventures in Wonderland. New York: Signet Classic, 1994.

Chilstrom, R. *God Awaits You*. Notre Dame, Ind.: Ave Maria Press, 1996.

Chopra, D. *Ageless Body, Timeless Mind*. New York: Crown, 1994.

Conybeare, F. C. "The Ring of Pope Xystus." First produced in London, 1910.

Covey, S. *First Things First Every Day*. New York: Fireside, 1997.

De Mello, A. *Awakening: The Perils and Opportunities of Reality*. New York: Bantam Doubleday, 1990.

De Mello, A. *Awareness*. New York: Doubleday, 1992.

Drucker, P. *Managing the Non-Profit Organization: Principles and Practice*. New York: HarperCollins, 1990.

Edison, T. Quoted in *Columbia World of Quotations*. New York: Columbia University Press, 1996.

Gillman, N. *Sacred Intentions: Daily Inspiration to Strengthen the Spirit, Based on Jewish Wisdom*. New York: Jewish Light, 1999.

Goa, D. J., Distad, L., and Wangler, M. *Anno Domini: Jesus Through the Centuries—Exploring the Heart of Two Millennia*. (Gallery guide.) Edmonton, Alberta, Canada: Provincial Museum, 2000.

Greenleaf, R. K. *The Servant as Leader*. Indianapolis: Robert K. Greenleaf Center, 1991.

Hanh, T. N. *Living Buddha, Living Christ*. New York: Putnam/Berkeley, 1997.

Havel, V. Address by president of the Czech Republic to the U.S. Congress, April 23, 1999.

International Religious Foundation (eds.). *World Scripture*. St. Paul, Minn.: Paragon House, 1995.

Janeway, E. *Elizabeth Jowett*. Quoted in Columbia World of Quotations. New York: Columbia University Press, 1996.

Jones, L. B. *The Path: Creating Your Mission Statement for Work and for Life*. New York: Hyperion, 1996.

Jones, T. "CT Classic: Frederick Buechner's Sacred Journey." Article on Christianity Today Website: http://www.christianitytoday.com/ct/ 2003/109/51.0.html.

Keating, T. *Open Heart, Open Mind: The Contemplative Dimension of the Gospel*. New York: HarperCollins, 2000.

Lama Surya Das. *Awakening to the Sacred: Creating a Spiritual Life from Scratch*. New York: Broadway Books, 2000.

Larson, D., Larson, S., and Koenig, H. "Research Findings on Religious Commitment and Mental Health." *Psychiatric Times*, Oct. 2003. Quote from *Psychiatric Times* Website: http://www.psychiatrictimes.com/ p.001078.htm.

Lasswell, M. "Defying the Laws of Comedy." *USA Weekend*, May 23, 2003.

Lawrence, Brother. *The Practice of the Presence of God*. New York: Barnes and Noble, 2000.

Lewis, C. S. *The Screwtape Letters*. New York: Touchstone, 1961.

Lusseyran, J. *Against the Pollution of the I*. New York: Parabola Books, 1999.

Mandus, Brother. *The Divine Awakening*. Evesham, UK: Arthur James, 1961.

McGinn, B. *The Flowering of Mysticism: Men and Women in the New Mysticism*. New York: Crossroad/Herder & Herder, 2001.

McManis, S. "There Was No Place Like Home: Lauralee Summer's Difficult Journey from Homeless to Harvard." *San Francisco Chronicle*, May 25, 2003.

Merton, T. *The New Seeds of Contemplation*. New York: New Directions, 1961.

Miller, T. *How to Want What You Have*. New York: Avon Books, 1995.

Newberg, A., and d'Aquili, E. *Why God Won't Go Away*. New York: Ballantine, 2001.

Osmond, M. "Aim High, Dream Big with 2 Million Words." *HardNewsCafe*, University of Utah, Aug. 30, 2000.

Pagels, E. *The Gnostic Gospels*. New York: Vintage Books, 1979.

Paul, J. *Becoming Your Own Hero*. Berkeley: Author, 2002.

Phillips-Jones, L. *Creating or Revisiting Your Personal Vision*. Quote from the Mentoring Group Website: http://www.mentoringgroup.com/ personalv1.htm-8k.

Rather, D. News feature on Chris Gardner. "CBS Evening News," May 2001.

Rause, V. "The Science of God: Searching for the Divine." *Readers Digest*, Dec. 2001.

Ritz, D. O. "Service to Others as Prayer." *Mind and Heart*. Newsletter. Sarasota, Fla.: Aug. 1993.

Rogers, Fred. Quoted on "MSN Chat," Oct. 12, 1999.

Roof, W. C. *The Christian Century*. Oct. 11, 2000.

Ryley, N. *The Forsaken Garden: Four Conversations and the Deep Meaning of Environmental Illness*. Wheaton, Ill.: Quest Books, 1998.

Singer, J. *A Gnostic Book of Hours: Keys to Inner Wisdom*. San Francisco: HarperSanFrancisco, 1992.

Southern, R., and Norton, R. *Cracking Your Congregation's Code: Mapping Your Spiritual DNA to Create Your Future*. San Francisco: Jossey-Bass, 2001.

Steindl-Rast, D. *Gratefulness Is the Heart of Prayer: An Approach to Life in Fullness*. Ramsey, N.J.: Paulist Press, 1984.

Taylor, J. "Jean's Story." Quoted from Website of Union Church of Cupertino, Calif.: www.unionchurch.org.jeansmiracle.htm, also /jeansmiracle2.htm.

"Teacher Plans a Gift of Gratitude." *Washington Times*. Article quoted from Website of *Christianity Today*: www.christianitytoday.com/ct/2002/109.21.0.htm.

Trueblood, D. E. *A Life of Search*. Richmond, Ind.: Friends United Press, 1996.

Vonnegut, K., Jr. *Timequake*. New York: Vintage, 1998.

Ware, C. *Discover Your Spiritual Type: A Guide to Individual and Congregational Growth*. New York: Alban Institute, 1995.

Watts, A. *The Wisdom of Insecurity*. New York: Random House, 1968.

Wilber, K. *One Taste: The Journals of Ken Wilber*. Boston: Shambala, 1999.

Winik, L. "Now I Want to Do Everything." *Parade*, May 25, 2003.

Wuthnow, R. *After Heaven: Spirituality in America Since the 1950s*. Berkeley: University of California Press, 2000.

THE AUTHORS

Robert Norton and *Richard Southern* have "morphed" themselves a number of times in their career paths. Robert Norton has been an elementary school teacher, a banker, and a marketing executive, and is now a consultant for faith-based nonprofit organizations.

Richard Southern has been a school principal, marketing executive, and gerontologist and is now also a consultant for faith-based nonprofits. He holds a Ph.D. from Claremont University.

In both of their lives, there has been a single consistent strand: a compelling interest in religion and spiritual practices. This shared interest resulted in their joint founding, in 1990, of Church Development Systems, a nonprofit organization. Their work with hundreds of faith communities and with thousands of spiritual leaders and seekers led them to create the processes that are included in this book.

They have been featured in the print media, on radio, and on television in the United States, Canada, Germany, Japan, and Australia. They both reside in the San Francisco Bay Area and are coauthors of *Cracking Your Congregation's Code: Mapping Your Spiritual DNA to Create Your Future* (Jossey-Bass, 2001).

INDEX

A

Abraham, 120
After Heaven (Wuthnow), xv
Against the Pollution of the I (Lusseyran), 107
Ageless Body, Timeless Mind (Chopra), 104
The Agony and the Ecstasy (film), 122–123
Alcoholics Anonymous, 123–124
Alcott, L. M., 51
Alice in Wonderland (Carroll), 52–53
Anchoring, and Life Map, 145
Anchorites, 83
Apocalypse, Cave of, 84–85
Armstrong, L., 54–55
Artress, L., 91
Assessment: and Circle of Life, 142–143; for heart-centered soul type, 76; for mind-centered soul type, 114; for soul-centered soul type, 96; for strength-centered soul type, 130–131
Augustine, Saint, 15
Awareness (De Mello), 112–113
Awareness, practice of, 99–116

B

Band Against MS Foundation, 108
Barker, J., 53

Bass, E., 10
Beattie, M., 72–73
Becoming Your Own Hero (Paul), 69
"Beliefnet" (Internet column), 72
Bojaxhiu, A., 124
Bonhoeffer, D., 73
Brackett, J., 92
Buddha, 93–94, 117, 120–121
Buddhism: contemplation and, 93–94; definition of soul in, 14; gratitude and, 72; Zen Buddhism, 94, 104
Buechner, F., 136

C

"Calvin and Hobbes," 107
Cameron, J., 7
Campbell, J., 149
Carrey, J., 106–107
Carroll, L., xv, 52–53
Cave of the Apocalypse, 84–85
Center for Positive Living, 129
Centering prayer, 86–87
Chant, 89
Charles, J., 125
Chartres Cathedral, and labyrinths, 91
Chilstrom, R., 94
Chopra, D., 104
Christ, and Buddha, 93–94
Christianity: definition of soul in, 15; monasticism and, 83

Cicero, 67

Circle of Life, 142–143

Commitment, practice of, 117–132

Confucius, 9

Contemplation, practice of, 79–98

Core values: approaches in identification of, 29–31; clarification of, 31–32; and Life Map construction, 138–139; listing of, 34–36; living in harmony with, 26–27; prioritization of, 32–33; repetition and, 146; review of, 147–148; worksheet for, 33

Covey, S., 38–39

Creating or Revising Your Personal Vision (Phillips-Jones), 52

Cross-cultural emphasis, and retreats, 86

D

Daily Word (magazine), 103–104

Dance, sacred, 92–93

D'Aquili, E., 5

De Mello, A., 112–113

Disney, W., 56

Drucker, P., 44

Dukes, B., 68–69

E

Eccles, J., 101

Eckhart Society, 94

Ecumenism, 86, 89

Einstein, A., 4

F

1 Chronicles 4:9–11, 17–18

1 Corinthians 13, 32

First Things First (Covey), 38–39

Francis of Assisi, Saint, 111–112

Frank, A., 73

Franklin, B., 26

G

Gandhi, M., 27

Gardner, C., 37–38

Genesis, and definition of soul, 14–15

Geometry, sacred, 90–92

Gillman, N., 84

The Gnostic Gospels (Pagels), 106

"The God Ad" campaign, 102

God Awaits You (Chilstrom), 94

God, names for, 19–20

God's Will, acceptance of, 108–109

Gratitude, practice of, 67–77

Greenleaf, R. K., 124–125

H

Hanh, T. N., 93–94

Heart-centered soul type, xviii, 7–8, 67–77

Hebrew scriptures, and definition of soul, 14–15

Herman, N., 110

Hinduism, and definition of soul, 14

Holmes, T., 74–75

The Horse Whisperer (film), 60

How to Want What You Have (Miller), 102–103

Human Genome Project, xvi, 6

I

Inamori, K., 118

Islam. *See* Muslims

Islamic mysticism. *See* Sufism

J

Jabez, 17–18

Janeway, E., 80

Jerry Maguire (film), 41–42

Jesus: contemplation and, 81; gratitude and, 71; names for, 21–22; servant leadership and, 125; spriritual journey and, 9

John 13:1–6, 125

John, Saint, 84–85

John the Baptizer, 81

Jones, L. B., 41

Jubus, 94

Judaism: contemplation and, 94; definition of soul in, 14–15

Judge, M., 126–127

Julius (pope), 122–123

Jung, C., xv, 65, 123–124

K

Keating, T., 86–87
Knight, A., 68–69
Knight, D., 68–69
Koans (stories from Zen Buddhism),
    104
Krishnamurti, J., 87

L

Labyrinth, as sacred geometry, 90–92
Lama Surya Das, 10
Lao Tzu, 23
Lawrence, Brother, 110
Lectio Divina (sacred reading), 88
Lew, A., 94
Lewis, C.S., 81
Liar, Liar (film), 106–107
Life Map: construction of, xix,
    135–148; values worksheet for, 33
Life Map Notes: importance of names
    and, 16–17; preparation for, 11; pur-
    pose statement and, 46–50; sacred
    names and, 22; vision statement
    and, 60–63
Listening, and awareness, 110–112
Living Buddha, Living Christ (Thich),
    93–94
Longfellow, H. W., 39–40
Luke 22:46, 99
Lusseyran, J., 107
Luther, M., 121–122

M

Maimonides, M., 4
Mandela, N., 82
Mandus, Brother, 109
Mark 5:24, 111
Maslow, A., 37
Master Unmon, 9
Matthew 11:15, 111
Matthew 25:40, 119
May, G., 10
McGinn, B., 94–95
Mekilta to Exodus, 20.20, 72
Merton, T., 9
Metanoia, and awareness, 106–110

Michelangelo, 122–123
Midrashic teaching, and gratitude, 72
Miller, T., 102–103
Mind-centered soul type, xviii, 8,
    99–116
"Mister Rogers' Neighborhood" (tele-
    vision program), 128
Mohammed, 82, 121
Monasticism, 83
Monkey mind, 111
Moses, 81–82
Mother Teresa, 124
Movement, sacred, 89–90
Mr. Holland's Opus (film), 39
Muslims, 9, 15, 92–93
Mysticism, 15, 81–82, 92–93

N

Names: for God, 19–20, 138; impor-
    tance of, 16–22; power of, 21–22
Neurotheology, 5
New Thought, 103–104, 129
Newberg, A., 4–6
Norman, M., 127–128
Numbers 12:5–6, 57

O

One Taste (Wilber), 32
Open Heart, Open Mind (Keating),
    86–87

P

Pagels, E., 106
Paradigm shift, and awareness,
    105–110
Partnering, 146–147
The Path (Jones), 41
Patmos (Greek island), 84–85
Paul, J., 69
Paul of Tarsus, 9, 32
Peace Pilgrim, 127–128
Pennington, B., 86–87
People of Israel, 9
Personal purpose statement, writing
    of, 43–45
Phillips-Jones, L., 52

Pope, A., 3
The Power of Vision (Barker), 53
The Practice of the Presence of God (Lawrence), 110
Practices: for heart-centered soul type, 77; for mind-centered soul type, 115–116; for soul-centered soul type, 97–98; and soul type, 143–145; for spiritual checkups, 146–147; for strength-centered soul type, 132
Protestant Reformation, and definition of soul, 15
Psyche (soul), 15
Purpose statement: development of, 37–43; and Life Map construction, 140; repetition and, 146; review of, 148; writing of, 43–50

Q

Qu'ran, 72

R

Ralston, A., 73–74
Reading, sacred, 88
Reeve, C., 19
Religion, and science, 3–4
Repetition, and Life Map, 146
Retreats, spiritual, 82–84, 86, 147–148
Revelation, Book of, 84–85
Revere, P., 39–40
A Review of the Lessons of Love (Beattie), 72–73
Ritz, D. O., 129
Roberts, M., 59–60
Rogers, F., 128, 129
Romans 12:2, 103
Roof, W. C., 9
Ruh (soul), 15
Rumi, M. J., 92–93

S

Sacred dance, 92–93
Sacred geometry, 90–92
Sacred Intentions (Gillman), 84
Sacred movement, 89–90

Sacred reading, 88
Sacred sound, 89
Science, and religion, 3–4
Self-talk, positive, 147
September 11, 2001, 41, 72, 126–127
The Servant as Leader (Greenleaf), 124–125
Servant leadership, 124–125
Shakers, 92
Shoemaker, S., 123–124
Siddhartha, Prince, 120–121
Simon Stylites, 83
Simons, M., 41
Simple Gifts shuffle, 92
Sistine Chapel, 122–123
Smedes, L., 72
Smith Agency, and "The God Ad" campaign, 102
Smith, B., 123–124
Smith, H., 3, 15
Sophocles, 13
Soul-centered soul type, xviii, 8, 79–98
Soul, definition of, 14–15
Sound, sacred, 89
Spiritual identity, clarification of, 137–138
Spiritual journey, reflection on, 8–10
Spirituality, definition of, 9–10
Sri Aurobindo, 9, 14
Steindl-Rast, D., 72
Strength-centered soul type, xviii, 8, 117–132
Sufism, 15, 92–93
Summer, L., 18–19
Sutton, M., 84–85

T

Taizé community (France), 89
Taylor, J., 108–109
Teresa of Avila, Saint, 135
Thich N. H., 93–94
Thoreau, H. D., 58
Timequake (Vonnegut), 70
Transformation, and awareness, 105–110
Trueblood, E., 25

U

Unity, 104
Upanishads, The, 65

V

Values. *See* Core values
Vision statement: creating of, 60–63;
  definition of vision and, 53–60; Life
  Map construction and, 141–142;
  repetition and, 146; review of, 148
Vonnegut, K., 70

W

Walker, C., 107–108
Ware, C., 10
Watts, A., 103

Wesley, J., 109–110
Wilber, K., 32
Williams, D., 80
Wilson, B., 123–124
The Wisdom of Insecurity (Watts), 103
Withdrawal, for contemplation,
  82–84
The Wizard of Oz (Baum), 133
Wordsworth, W., 79
World Trade Center attack, 41, 72,
  126–127
Wuthnow, R., xv, 123–124

Z

Zen Buddhism, 94, 104. *See also*
  Buddhism